BEFORE
THE
STORM

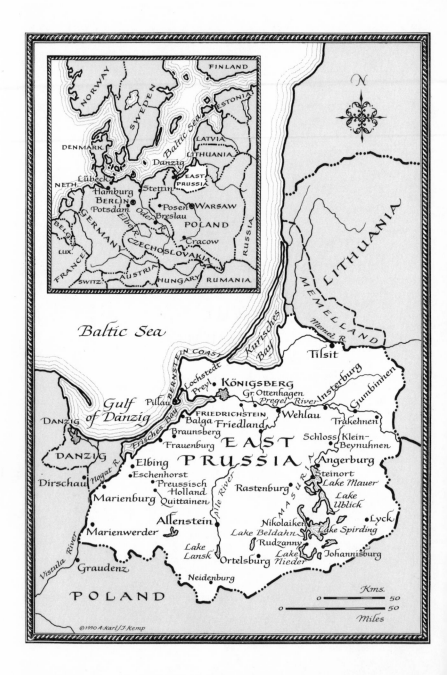

N

FINLAND

NORWAY

SWEDEN

Baltic Sea

ESTONIA

LATVIA

LITHUANIA

DENMARK

Danzig

EAST
PRUSSIA

NETH.

Lübeck

Stettin

Hamburg

BERLIN

Potsdam

Posen

WARSAW

BELG.

GERMANY

Oder R.

Elbe R.

Breslau

POLAND

RUSSIA

LUX.

FRANCE

SWITZ.

CZECHOSLOVAKIA

Cracow

AUSTRIA

HUNGARY

RUMANIA

Baltic Sea

LITHUANIA

MEMELLAND

Memel R.

Kurisches Bay

Tilsit

BERNSTEIN COAST

Lochstedt

Preyl

Königsberg

Gr. Ottenhagen

Pregel River

Insterburg

Gumbinnen

Pillau

*Gulf
of Danzig*

Frisches Bay

FRIEDRICHSTEIN

Wehlau

Trakehnen

DANZIG

Balga

Friedland

Braunsberg

DANZIG

Nogat R.

Frauenburg

E A S T

Schloss Klein-
Beynuhnen

Dirschau

Elbing

P R U S S I A

Angerburg

Eschenhorst

Steinort

Preussisch
Holland

Rastenburg

Lake Mauer

Marienburg

Quittainen

Nile River

*Lake
Ublick*

Masuria

Marienwerder

Allenstein

Nikolaiken

Lake Spirding

Lyck

Vistula River

Lake Beldahn

Rudzanny

*Lake
Lansk*

Ortelsburg

*Lake
Nieder*

Johannisburg

Graudenz

Neidenburg

P O L A N D

Kms.

0   50

0   50

Miles

©1990 A.Karl/J.Kemp

Marion, Countess Dönhoff

BEFORE THE STORM

MEMORIES OF MY YOUTH IN OLD PRUSSIA

Translated by Jean Steinberg

Alfred A. Knopf ⬥ New York 1990

$\mathscr{C}$ONTENTS

OREWORD

George F. Kennan

The geographic entity known historically as East Prussia, a territory somewhat larger than the state of Maryland, was conquered and colonized in the thirteenth century by the Teutonic Order, and remained, with some intervals of Polish conquest, German down to the end of the Second World War—after 1701 a part of the Kingdom of Prussia; later, from 1871 to 1919, of the German Reich; then finally, from 1919 to 1933, of Weimar Germany. Its southeastern reaches contained a large area of heavily forested and beautiful lake districts, much of the remainder of the province consisting of rich and well-cultivated farming country, including a considerable number of large and highly productive estates. Some idea of its fertility may be gained from the fact that it was supporting, on the eve of the Second World War, some 1.5 million head of cattle and nearly 2 million pigs, not to mention a half a million horses, among them many of Europe's finest.

The Second World War brought with it a wide spectrum of sufferings and disasters: immense loss of human life, great displacements of innocent civilian populations, massive destruction of material values. One did not have to go

to East Prussia to look for that sort of thing—a number of
cities, in particular, suffered terrible destruction; but it is
hard to think of any other entire region of such size,
anywhere, that suffered so sweeping, indeed almost total, a
disaster, any that had so much to lose and lost so much of it,
as this ill-fated territory. When the tide of war had swept
over it in the terrible winter of 1944–45, the region was, to
anyone who had known it before, scarcely recognizable—a
single great field of devastation, parts of it almost devoid of
human inhabitants. Its few cities had been terribly destroyed. Its agricultural infrastructure was in ruins. Most of
the people, some 1,750,000 of them in fact, had fled to the
west—fled under conditions of danger and hardship that
would be difficult, today, to imagine. Of those who remained many were killed or deported to Siberia. (The rest
were expelled in 1950.) And in the provisional settlements
that followed in the end of hostilities, this ravaged and
nearly deserted territory was abandoned, so far as the
western allies were concerned, to the Communist con-
querors, left to be divided between the Russians and the
Poles and to remain that way down to the present day. There
is no evidence that anything even resembling its former
civilizational infrastructure and prosperity has ever been
restored.

Among the victims of this tragedy there were none for
whom the disaster was more extensive, more heart-rending,
and more final than for the large landed estates. Almost all
of the manor houses, some of them structures of great
historical and aesthetic value, appear to have been, whether
by deliberate design or otherwise, burned to the ground,

carrying with them to destruction all of the rare works of art, antiquities, and libraries that so many of them housed. Think as one may about the sociological and economic qualities of this form of land tenure, judge as one may the qualities of the societies and the persons that supported it, what occurred to places of this nature during the war, in East Prussia and elsewhere, represented a grievous impairment of the historical and cultural heritage of European civilization.

It was on one of these East Prussian estates, and in just such a manor house (one of the greatest and finest of them, in fact) that the childhood and early youth of the woman who wrote this book were passed. She was destined, after a considerable absence at various universities, to return to these familiar places before the war and there, with almost all of the male family members who could have taken over this function gone (they were, almost to a man, killed in battle or executed by the Nazi authorities), to administer the agricultural operations of two of these great estates. She bore this responsibility to the very end, to the point where the advancing Soviet forces were only hours away and where no choice remained for her but to do what she actually did: to mount a horse, to join the endless road-clogging columns of fugitives, and to ride seven hundred miles in zero weather (this took her some seven weeks) to the relative safety of the defeated and semidestroyed non-Communist Germany of the west. From that, she went on to become a journalist and writer of distinction, among other things initially editor and now publisher of the well-known Hamburg weekly *Die Zeit.*

So sweeping, so definitive, was the expunging of the civilization Marion Dönhoff was leaving behind her in East Prussia that there is a problem, now, in preserving the very historical memory of it. Of the visible ruins and other relics that normally serve to remind us of past civilizations less would seem to have survived in the case of East Prussia than of civilizations that reached their high points centuries in the past. Almost the only bonds that may now link the earlier life of that East Prussian region with the consciousness of people of later generations are the memories of those who participated in that life and are capable of recording for posterity what they remembered of it.

This, we may be sure, was one of the factors Marion Dönhoff had in mind as she set out to commit her own reminiscences to paper, and thus to make them available to the later generations. In doing so, she has made a serious contribution to the history of this troubled century, and one that will be appreciated by all those who are inclined to examine and to ponder the immediate historical background of the Europe we now have before us.

BEFORE
THE
STORM

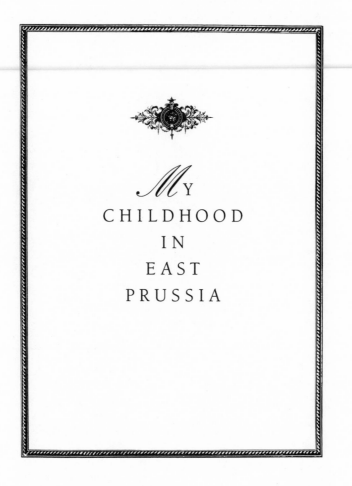

My
CHILDHOOD
IN
EAST
PRUSSIA

$\mathcal{F}$RIEDRICHSTEIN

The children of my brother who was killed in the war invented a game that posed the question "How many handshakes separate you from— —?" The responder had to name a person, preferably someone renowned who had lived in the long-ago and preferably historic past.

I was in a position to win over all the other players because my father was sixty-four years old when I was born, and his father forty-eight when he himself was born. In other words, my grandfather was born in 1797, which gave me a significant advantage in our parlor game. My grandfather had been a diplomat and sometime foreign minister, a sophisticated, educated man, the intimate of artists and scholars, and thus I had no difficulty in establishing that no more than three handshakes stood between me and Humboldt, Schadow, Rauch, and Goethe.

Perhaps it was this game that made me aware of the time span separating me from the past that shaped me—not only in sheer length of time but also with regard to its sociological and cultural levels. The tendrils of the *ancien régime* reached to the threshold of my childhood, for until the end

of the First World War—I was then not yet ten years old—
Germany in effect was still a semifeudal society.

The continuing role of the nobility in both the government and the military hierarchy gave ample proof of this. At
the outbreak of the First World War, all commanders of
the eighteen Prussian and German army corps came
from the ranks of the nobility, and even in the declining
days of the monarchy eleven of the thirteen presidents of the
Prussian provinces—the highest administrative officials—
were noblemen. All ambassadors (a mere nine at the time,
because the German Reich was represented by ambassadors
only in the most important states) were members of the
nobility, and of the thirty-eight envoys representing the
Foreign Office in the smaller countries, only four were
commoners. One of these, Ulrich Rauscher, was the chief
diplomatic representative at Warsaw. When an uncle of
mine was appointed Rauscher's legation counselor in 1922,
I remember hearing serious discussions about whether a
man who did not come from the ranks of the nobility could
really master all the nuances of diplomacy—its tradition,
style, and tact.

Obviously, the conscious or unconscious prejudices of
interested parties dominate the way people think. Who at
that time among these people would have imagined that
Jews one day would make outstanding soldiers and superb
farmers? Often it is not facts but perceptions of facts that
matter in history.

My older brothers and sisters had already reached the age
of reason at the time of the First World War, and so for me
they represented a link between "before" and the new age.

The new age, my age, began with the end of the monarchy and the birth of the democratic era. The era before the First World War, even though it was not all that distant, I knew only from the accounts of others.

I came across a telling illustration of such reminiscences in the memoirs of Otto von Hentig, father of the well-known educator Hartmut von Hentig. Otto von Hentig, born in 1886, was a diplomat who gained fame through his adventurous "journey into the closed land," Afghanistan, which he undertook in 1915 at the behest of the Foreign Office. In his account, Hentig tells of a family visit to my ancestral home, Friedrichstein:

Friedrichstein Castle, built in 1709–14, was one of East Prussia's three most significant structures of its kind. The Italianate rococo plasterwork of its reception rooms dated back to 1750.

It must have been in the summer of 1902 when we visited the castle, then still run in grand style, for the second time. In Königsberg we were met by a carriage drawn by four horses, and an accompanying baggage cart. The parents again were given the royal suite; that is to say, the rooms set aside for the Prussian kings when they visited East Prussia. Frederick William I, Frederick the Great, and both Frederick William II and IV had stayed there. We children were given the adjoining back rooms.

Immediately after Count August finished conducting the morning services in the presence of about twenty in part very attractive young housemaids dressed in pink uniforms, as well as the head butler and the two assistant footmen, the excellent breakfast was served on a huge silver platter. Every evening [there were] formal dinners with guests from the neighboring houses and from Königsberg, not to mention the constant stream of visitors from the world of diplomacy, the upper nobility, and the intellectual elite.

Except for the number of housemaids, which, it seems to me, grew exponentially in Otto Hentig's imagination, I could in my childhood still bear witness to the accuracy of his account: the four-horse carriage and the morning services, although in my time they were conducted by my mother, not by my father. We still had Kadow, the head butler, very dignified in black suit or tailcoat, and his two assistants in light-colored striped linen jackets or, on festive occasions, in black breeches, red stockings, red shoes with silver buckles, and frocklike coats. The six housemaids we still had in my childhood all wore pink-and-white-striped dresses; the three kitchen maids, however, were exempted from this passion for liveries.

Incidentally, among the lower ranks the hierarchies were as rigid as among the dignitaries at court. The cook would never have sat down to eat with the kitchen maids, nor the housekeeper with the housemaids; the cook and the house-keeper ate in a separate room at a table to which only my mother's maid and possibly an unmarried adjunct of the inspector, the so-called *élève,* were admitted. The three assistant coachmen who served under the head coachman also ate in the castle. They too had their own table, although theirs was in a passageway.

The housemaids and the assistant coachmen all came from the village or, as the people called it, the earldom— that is, from one of its estates. The fact that in this part of the world industry was still in its infancy, and consequently the chance of finding jobs in the city was scant, explains the ready availability of so many servants. Moreover, service in the castle was far preferred to farm labor. Even though wages were not high, the advantages—light work, housing, clothing, and food—were important considerations.

It was still a largely moneyless economy. Most farmhands were paid in kind: houses, firewood, grain for breadmaking and hog fodder, as well as milk or a piece of land for potatoes. In one form or another potatoes played a big role in rural life. One of the greatest pleasures of my childhood was helping Master Klein, our carpenter, or some other special friend with his fall potato harvest. The best part came at the end, when the dry potato tops were piled up and burned and gray clouds of smoke wafted over the land as from sacrificial offerings. Then we would be overcome by an indefinable, ineradicable autumnal feeling of sadness. Even now, when I see the depiction of such a scene in the East, I cannot help feeling homesick.

$\mathscr{A}$ VISIT BY HINDENBURG

The four older siblings in our family — two brothers and two sisters — were between ten and six years older than I. At the age of seventeen my oldest brother volunteered for service in the First World War. I was the youngest of the three "little ones": my brother Christoph, who was three years older than I; a sickly sister, who had a private nurse; and I.

The only thing I myself remember about the First World War is Hindenburg's week-long visit to Friedrichstein in 1916. When Russia invaded East Prussia in mid-August, 1914, we children, in the very first days of the war, were packed off to Saxony, to my mother's sister, the wife of a Mr. von Helldorff, and were not brought back home until Hindenburg recaptured East Prussia from the Russians at the

Battle of Tannenberg a fortnight later. The hero of that battle was the renowned Field Marshal General von Hindenburg.

The victory itself soon became the stuff of legend, and we children were told how the Russians had become mired in the Masurian swamps. In my mind's eye I could see the soldiers stuck helplessly in the bog, and of course I felt very

In 1916, Field Marshal Hindenburg spent a week at Friedrichstein. Mother and the "victor of Tannenberg" in front of the church at Löwenhagen.

sorry for them. Ninety thousand Russian prisoners were taken at Tannenberg, apparently the only battle of encirclement fought in the Great War. It must have been a brilliant military coup. Of the eight German armies, seven had been deployed on the Western Front, which meant that only a single one had been available in East Prussia to face the far stronger Russian forces.

Hindenburg had retired in 1911, and it was said that when he was hastily called back in 1914—he was then sixty-seven—he had not even managed to lay his hands on an official field-gray uniform; he showed up in East Prussia in a sort of simple tunic. When he came to Friedrichstein, I was extremely disappointed because he looked nothing like the way I had pictured him. A tall heavyset man, he walked with a rather stiff gait and oddly short steps, and with his mustache he looked more like the Nutcracker in one of my picture books than the heroic figure of my imagination.

At Home
AND ABROAD

The group that gathered around our table at mealtime was large, mainly because living in the country we children were all taught at home. That meant tutors, governesses, and a French mistress. The assemblage also included my father's secretary and another permanent guest, my mother's friend Edith von Zedlitz, a humorless spinster who stuck her nose into everything and, much to our chagrin, took it upon herself to issue a constant stream of behavioral guidelines.

Fired up by war fervor, Edith Zedlitz carried frugality to extremes. Thus we were not allowed to put both butter and jam on our bread, and she was incredibly inventive about finding substitutes for any number of products: ersatz coffee made out of acorns we children had to gather; shoe polish made from lampblack scraped from one of our fireplaces; soap made out of heaven only knows what.

The poverty of those early postwar years is mind-boggling to me now, as I recall it. People with backpacks would come from the cities to glean stray spikes of grain in the fields, take them home, thresh and grind them as best they could. The villagers wore wooden clogs, except at church on Sunday, when they would carry their shoes in their hands, put them on at the church door, and change back into their clogs when leaving. We too became very frugal. We never traveled second class on the railroad (first class was not to be thought of), but sat on the hard wooden benches of third class, even for trips as long as from Königsberg to Berlin.

After 1918 the number of people at our dining table was swelled by a constant stream of Russian émigrés and Baltic refugees. Most of them stayed only briefly, except for the Lievens: Prince Lieven, a quiet, distinguished man, his somewhat eccentric but extremely witty wife, and their five children—Egon, Sigrid, Nicol, Marieluise, and Joachim—who lived with us for years.

Joachim suffered a particularly tragic fate. When I managed our estates in the Second World War, I was able to persuade the authorities to exempt him from military service because he, as my only male assistant—all my brothers were serving in the war—was indispensable in the administration of the estates. But in the final phases of the war even that argument no longer proved effective, and without being given a hearing he was assigned to a Waffen SS unit, a hard blow for so fervent an anti-Nazi. A letter he wrote in January, 1945, from the Kolmar region was the last word we ever had from him.

My older brothers and sisters all had tutors, governesses, and language teachers, including my brother Christoph, who spoke French before he spoke German. The "big ones" treated him just as badly as they treated me, which once led him to exclaim, *"Oh, comme je suis malheureux dans cette maison!"*

By the time I came of school age the situation had radically changed, either because of postwar conditions or perhaps because by the time my parents got around to their seventh child they had lost interest in her education. At any rate, my schooling was left more or less to chance. From time to time my father's secretary would take me under her wing, and at other times one of our young Baltic visitors or one of my older siblings would pitch in. Naturally, nothing useful could come out of this sort of instruction.

Finally it was decided to rent an apartment in Königsberg, and those of us still of school age were sent off under the watchful eye of Uncle Paul Below and Aleh, my beloved governess. This interlude soon came to an end, for reasons not entirely clear to me. The only thing I was told was that the school there did not care to have me any longer. The classes were overcrowded and I was invariably late; possibly the combination of these factors prompted the decision.

My lateness was connected with the "cooking box," a contraption I suspect of having been one of Edith Zedlitz's legacies. In theory, this box, which contained a padded lining, was supposed to save fuel. In the evening you would put parboiled mush, generally barley or groats, into the box, and by next morning the food was supposed to be cooked to perfection. However, perfection does not begin to describe the result. The almost raw, thick groats were so disgusting that I was unable to swallow them. This led to interminable dawdling at the breakfast table, and consequently to chronic lateness.

And so after a few months, shortly before my ninth birthday, I returned to Friedrichstein with Aleh, my brief excursion into the big world of Königsberg at an end. I had mixed feelings when I boarded the train to Löwenhagen, where Grenda, our head coachman, was waiting for us at the station in his two-horse carriage.

When Grenda went to meet my parents at Löwenhagen, he would be dressed in his elegant brown livery and black bowler. He would touch the brim of his hat with his right thumb and forefinger, a pose he held without moving or changing his expression until everyone was in the carriage.

Then he would take off at a lively pace, the wheels of the coach bouncing from paving stone to paving stone, producing a clatter that once heard is never forgotten.

Of course, Aleh and I were not worthy of so grand a reception. Grenda met us perched on the driver's seat wearing an old jacket and grinning from ear to ear. Why? I asked myself worriedly. Did he perhaps think I'd been booted out of school? Grenda was a stickler for hierarchic gradations. He would have been eminently well qualified to give us lessons in matters of protocol, although that was not necessary since one could always guess his feelings.

At a rapid pace we traveled along the tree-lined road from Löwenhagen to Friedrichstein, then down the narrow

The lake in front of Friedrichstein.

defile, with the lake on the left and the castle to the right in front of us. Back in the early eighteenth century—six generations before my time—the builder of Friedrichstein, Otto-Magnus Dönhoff, had chosen a magnificent site: a driveway fronting on a vast expanse of lawn and a long lake framed by wooded hills. The front of the house had only two stories while the rear, which faced the park, had three, because the terrain sloped down toward the valley of the Pregel River.

The heavy front door opened up into a great hall with three inner doors above which hung portraits of Frederick the Great's dogs, a gift to his hosts. To the left and the right stood two huge wardrobes. The center door led into an airy garden room with ornately plastered walls and ceiling.

The view from the balcony of Friedrichstein, across the wide, hedge-bordered lawn to the Pregel River meadows.

When important visitors were expected, all the doors were flung open: the heavy front door, the door to the garden room, and finally the tall double door from the garden room to the pillared balcony, with its view of a broad, hedge-lined lawn; from there two parallel tree-lined roads led down to the verdant infinity of the Pregel meadows. Visitors invariably reacted to this view in stunned admiration: "More beautiful than Versailles!" one of them exclaimed. And the effect of the view through the castle to the magnificently tended landscape was very special indeed.

Once again I began to be taught at home. I felt a bit lonely. Things livened up only on weekends, when my brothers and sisters came home from Königsberg. Then my youngest brother and I would climb up into the attic with its many secrets, which no one but the two of us ever explored. The attic extended over the entire length of the building, and in the nooks between the heavy beams we discovered all sorts of wonderful things, like piles of nets used in wolf hunts, for until the middle of the last century wolves, and even an occasional lynx, still prowled the countryside. We also found marvelous backdrops and old-fashioned props for the entertainments staged by our forebears, and a tablet decorated with oak leaves hailing the returning heroes—evidently to welcome home my father and his twin brother upon their return from the Franco-Prussian War in 1871.

With the help of a ladder we could climb up between the beams, almost up to the ridge of the roof, open a dormer window, and look out across the countryside. I thought this was one of the most beautiful spots in the house. Downstairs, in the ceremonial rooms, things were frightfully formal, and the many fragile porcelain and terra-cotta figurines hampered one's freedom of movement. But not in the so-called Little Foyer, adjacent to the big entrance hall, from which a wide, rather steep curved staircase led up to the royal suite. My big brothers had discovered that by using a tray like a sled, they could whizz down these stairs with great verve.

Our day was punctuated by numerous religious observances, beginning with the aforementioned morning service attended by the children and staff. This service opened with a chorale, accompanied on the harmonium by my oldest sister, followed by my mother's reading of a Psalm or a chapter of one of the Gospels, and closed with the Lord's Prayer. Grace was said at the beginning and end of every meal, usually by me, the youngest family member. Having taken over this obligation from my older brother, I had never seen a printed version of the prayer *"Komm, Herr Jesus, sei unser Gast . . ."* (Come, Lord Jesus, be our guest . . .). I knew it only from hearing it, and for a long time I wondered why a prayer would begin with a comma: *Komma Jesus, sei unser Gast . . .* I was apparently willing to accept anything I heard, however puzzling, and not ask questions, because that would only expose me to the ridicule of the grown-ups. I also wondered in vain who the Martha might be in the hymn *"Die wir uns allhier beisammen finden . . . ,"* the reason for my puzzlement being the phrase *"uns auf deine Marter zu verbinden, schlagen wird die Hände ein . . ."* (we join hands to share in your martyrdom . . .).

On Sundays we all attended church at Löwenhagen. The

proprietor of Friedrichstein was the traditional patron of the Löwenhagen church and, during my childhood, also of the Borchersdorf and Ottenhagen churches. With the sale of these two holdings to the community, the patronage, which carried with it obligations as well as rights, including the appointment of the pastor, also came to an end. In Löwenhagen the church patron and his family had special elevated pews that faced the pulpit, something like first-tier boxes with five or six red velvet upholstered chairs. The first chair, close to the organ, was the patron's, and the others were for the rest of the family.

Most of the time I understood very little of the sermon, and probably also did not listen, because it was far more interesting to watch what was going on. For example, I noticed how Father, while praying, would press his hat to his forehead and thus cover his face, and how one singer in the choir, a Miss Lunau, tended to open her mouth wide in fervent ecstasy. From my perspective—I was too short to peer over the railing—I could not see the pastor, but I could see the wood carving above the pulpit. When I tilted my head a bit the carving looked like a clown with a pointed cap. I was forever trying to see whether he was still there.

*M*Y FATHER

I hardly knew my father. He died in 1920, at the age of seventy-five, when I was barely ten. I still remember the day. It was a sunny September morning. The atmosphere in the house was very strange; everybody seemed very subdued. I can see myself sitting on a chair in the big parlor all alone, legs dangling, as the sun painted shadowy patterns on the parquet floor; except for the buzzing of a wasp everything was completely silent.

One of my older brothers said to me, "Father is dying, but you'd better stay here." Everyone was gathered around him except me; I, as usual, was "too little" and therefore excluded. I don't know what made me sadder, being shut out or the death of my father; of course I did not really grasp its significance.

My most vivid memory of Father is of him at his desk in the evening. His study was at the end of a suite of rooms that ran along the entire 250-foot side of the castle facing the park. The connecting doors of the rooms were always kept open, and so I could see him at the far end of the enfilade, sitting at his desk, illuminated by a lamp, like a beacon of light at the end of a long, dark tunnel.

There is much I could have learned from my father, an objective, thoughtful, and interested observer. I have been told that his friends called him "the man who wants to know everything." In addition to the many German newspapers of every shade of opinion to be found in his study, he also subscribed to *The Times*, *Le Temps*, and *Le Figaro*. When I saw him around the house during the day I made myself scarce, fearing he would ask me to read to him. His sight was failing, and, reluctant to burden his secretary yet eager to keep abreast of events, to learn what was in the three or

My father, August Karl Dönhoff, ex-diplomat, member of Prussia's Upper House from 1881 to 1903, and member of the Reichstag.

four newspapers that had not yet been read to him, he kept an eagle eye out for his children. The "big ones" also did not like being caught; they always had far more interesting things planned. For me, who could not yet read very well, it was torture when I failed to elude him and was forced to work my way painfully through articles I did not understand.

At the age of twenty-one my father had served in the 1866 war against Austria in the Royal Hussar regiment as a sergeant, and four years later as a reserve officer in the Franco-Prussian War. Immediately thereafter he entered the foreign service and was posted to the embassy in Paris as attaché. But diplomacy apparently did not appeal to him, for he left the foreign service after only ten years.

Recently, in the course of some research in the archives of the Foreign Office at Bonn, I came across material tracing his career, beginning with the day he was graduated from secondary school. It would appear that as a young man his work took him hither and yon: in 1874 he served as third councilor at Petersburg at an annual salary of 4,200 marks; subsequently he was sent to Vienna and London, and finally in 1878 he was appointed legation secretary in Washington at an annual salary of 10,800 marks.

Looking through the files, one gets the impression that he spent more time on leave—unpaid, to be sure—than at work. In 1873 he took time off to go to the Caucasus and southern Russia; in 1875 he went to Cuba, Mexico, Japan, and China, and immediately after that he took another year's leave. In March, 1881, he traveled again, and a letter from his regiment was forwarded by the Foreign Office to

Cairo, where he was expected. To judge by a marginal note written by Secretary of State von Bülow, Father seems to have extended his vacations arbitrarily: "Overstayed his leave without authorization," it says, like a reprimand on a school record.

In 1882 he informed the Foreign Office of his wish to resign, and in July he left his government post. He gave as a reason the fact that, having become a hereditary member of the Prussian Upper House upon the death of his father, he now wished to give his time to political affairs. His private life was devoted to his collection of objets d'art. He was in touch with antiquarians and museums the world over, particularly with Wilhelm Bode, the curator of Berlin's Kaiser Friedrich Museum. In the last decade of the nineteenth century, a fairly knowledgeable person was able to assemble a marvelous collection without a great deal of money.

My father traveled widely, which in his time was by no means as commonplace as it would be today. (Hard as it may be to believe, a man like Konrad Adenauer, who as Lord Mayor of Cologne and as a member of the Prussian legislature for decades before the Second World War played a fairly important role in German political life, was seventy before he first visited Paris and Rome, in his role as Federal Chancellor.) My father's globe-circling trips between 1875 and 1895 became a constant source of anxiety for the family he left behind; months would pass without news from him.

One day long after the Second World War when I was living in Hamburg as a journalist, a lady in Berlin telephoned to tell me of a find she had made in an antiques shop: a silver coffee pot with an engraving about someone by the name of Dönhoff. I wrote to the dealer and asked whether he would agree to let me have a look at it and, in case I was interested, to tell me its price. Soon thereafter the pot arrived; it turned out to be a Communion cup my grandmother—obviously in fulfillment of a pledge—had donated to her church in gratitude for the safe return of her oldest son from a journey. It was engraved with these words: "In memory of the blessed return of the church patron Count August Dönhoff from his around-the-world trip on May 24, 1881, given to the church at Borchersdorf by his grateful mother, Pauline, Countess Dönhoff, née Lehndorff." The cup had probably been stolen in East Prussia and come to Berlin during the war, and now, a hundred years after its presentation, had laboriously found its way back to me, the family representative.

This story has yet another curious twist. When the antiquarian mentioned a figure of DM 700, I told him that the price was agreeable to me and asked him for the name of his bank. There was no answer. I once again wrote to him requesting that he let me know where to send the money, and again there was no reply. Finally I asked the lady who had first told me about the cup if she would get me the information. It turned out that the shop no longer existed; its owner was bankrupt and nobody knew his whereabouts. Well, having done all I could to pay him, I decided it was only right that this loot should come back to the granddaughter of the donor without charge.

I deeply regret not knowing more about my father. It would have been so interesting to talk to him and to ask him questions, a man who had been both a member of the Prussian Upper House and a Reichstag deputy, a member of two institutions that represented two completely different eras, the old and the new, with the First World War as the line of demarcation. (The Prussian Upper House continued to function until the end of that war.) Someone who belonged to both at once must have been in a position to make highly interesting observations.

The Reichstag, chosen in universal, secret elections—unlike the Prussian legislature, which was the product of a three-tier electoral system—represented the modern era and the nascent industrial society. Even if politics in Germany, and foreign policy in particular, still lay largely outside the jurisdiction of Parliament, the new forces of the industrial state were given visible representation there. In the elections of 1912, the Social Democrats gained 110 seats in the Reichstag, which made them the strongest bloc even before the First World War.

Prussia's Upper House, on the other hand, was a symbol of the pre-industrial agrarian era. Here the nobility still enjoyed all the privileges of a class-based society. Moreover, the Prussian Upper House had neither parties nor blocs. Most of its members—including all the heads of the former ruling or princely families, as well as the proprietors of large estates—held hereditary seats. The landed gentry, organized in leagues, was also represented. It is safe to say that three-fourths of all its members came from the ranks of the nobility. The rest was recruited from among heads of ministries, high civil servants, generals, church dignitaries, and industrialists like Stumm, Siemens, and Krupp, this last category being appointed by the Emperor. In addition, the Prussian universities appointed ten delegates, and finally, the forty-nine Prussian cities sent one delegate each—among them, after 1917, Konrad Adenauer, Lord Mayor of Cologne. Golo Mann, in an essay entitled "The End of Prussia," writes: "I once asked the late Federal Chancellor, who, as a member of the Upper House and of Bonn's Parliament, must have witnessed his share of deliberative assembly sessions, which of the two, in his opinion, was on a higher plane. Adenauer's answer surprised me. 'The Prussian Upper House' was his reply."

With regard to my father's characteristic lack of social prejudice, I remember two stories my mother used to tell with some amusement. On the occasion of an official dinner at the Royal Palace in Berlin, she deemed it advisable to arrive earlier than the other guests since she was lady-in-waiting to the Empress. However, on that particular day she ran into a problem. As a rule, our family, including the head coachman, Grenda, and the horses and carriages, moved from East Prussia to Berlin for the Parliamentary session. I have no idea why on that evening neither Grenda nor his helper was there. Whatever the reason, it got later and later, until finally my father went out on the street, probably hoping for a lift from some other invited guest driving by. But the only vehicle he could see was a vegetable cart whose owner was returning home from market.

"My good man," said my father to the driver after asking him to stop, "could you take us to the Palace?" probably also adding that the man would not regret doing so. The driver was willing, and so my parents, both in formal dress, climbed on the cart and drove up to the Palace, doubtless to the great astonishment of the assembled guests.

The other story also had to do with the royal court. The morning after these parties, some of the guests—the Duke of Arenberg and the Duke of Ratibor and their wives, Prince and Princess Lichnowsky, and other such exalted personages—used to breakfast at the Hotel Adlon near the Brandenburg Gate. My father, who was always very busy and who had already enjoyed the company of these people the previous evening, had an appointment with a lawyer by the name of Silberstein, so he and my mother breakfasted at the Adlon with Silberstein. My mother, who was twenty years my father's junior, would have preferred more amusing company and kept looking longingly over to the other group; they for their part were probably somewhat surprised at my father's breakfast guest.

When I was little, I knew only one story about my father—a very exciting one, for it concerned his involvement in one of the last hostile confrontations between the Americans and the Indians. I had overheard my older brothers and sisters talk about it, but they ignored my excited questions, and I would never have dared ask my father directly. There was too great a distance between us. Many years later I read an account of the incident from the American perspective in Marshall Sprague's *Massacre: The Tragedy at White River.*

In September 1879, Carl Schurz, then United States Secretary of the Interior, was on an inspection tour of the Indian Agencies in the vicinity of Colorado Springs. Schurz, a Rhinelander by birth, had joined the German democratic movement as a student and fled Germany in 1849, after the revolution, first going to Switzerland, later to France and England, and ultimately emigrating to America in 1852. He was one of the earliest public figures to come out for the integration of Indians into American society.

My father, at the time on the staff of the German embassy at Washington, was a friend of Schurz and had arranged to meet him in Denver. Together they visited another fellow countryman, General Charles Adams. Adams, formerly Carl Schwanbeck and a native of Anklam in Pomerania, was in charge of safeguarding the post roads of Colorado and New Mexico. These three were joined by a son of President Hayes and by yet another of Schurz's friends, Walt Whitman, who had lost his job at the Department of the Interior after the publication of his *Leaves of Grass* in 1855.

The Ute Indian Reservation was in a fertile region coveted by its white neighbors; moreover, rich silver deposits had just been discovered in Leadville. This combination of fertile land and silver made for enormous tension, and finally led to a massacre of the whites of the Indian Agency by the Indians. Some were murdered, including the head of the Agency, and his wife and daughters were kidnapped.

Emotions ran high, and calls for military intervention and retribution went up. Schurz hurried back to Washington; he and General Adams were determined to do everything in their power to win the release of the women through negotiation, without resort to armed force.

As worried about the consequences of the massacre as Secretary Schurz, my father offered to help. He got on a horse and joined General Adams and his troops, apparently without a thought about what his superiors in Washington would say were they to hear of the involvement of a member of the German diplomatic delegation in this sort of derring-do. The expedition set out for the headquarters of the chief of the Utes on the Rio Grande. Theirs was a rugged trip over Indian trails, through gullies and riverbeds, up to elevations of ten thousand feet. They traveled for days before they found the Indian camp, and after lengthy negotiations the women were released unharmed. "Unharmed" was the crucial factor; it had been widely feared that they might have been raped, in which event nothing Schurz or anyone else could do would have prevented a bloody conflict with the Utes.

My MOTHER

As I mentioned earlier, my mother was lady-in-waiting to the Empress, which, I suspect, influenced her personal beliefs as well as some of our domestic practices—as, for example, the use of the phrase "most humbly," the salutation used in letters to the Emperor. "Most humbly, good morning, Your Excellency" was how the maids at Friedrichstein greeted my mother. The villagers—at any rate those to whom we had close and affectionate ties, like Mrs. Ott, the wife of a laborer, who taught my older sisters to weave and my mother to spin—said *Exzellenzchen* (Little Excellency). In East Prussia the diminutive suffix "chen" was appended to everything and everyone dear to one's heart, and we in turn called housemaids Bertchen, Annchen, Friedchen.

My mother had a number of siblings. One of her brothers lived in South America, then considered the end of the world. She addressed her own mother in the old-fashioned manner as *Frau Mutter,* and with the formal *Sie.* Mother spent part of her childhood at her grandparents' estate, Heiligenkreuz, in Croatia (now Yugoslavia). Once a year her parents traveled to Heiligenkreuz by horse carriage from Mecklenburg—heaven only knows how long that trip took.

My mother had an artistic bent. She was very imaginative and somewhat romantic. She had a pleasant singing voice, wrote charming little fairy tales as a pastime, painted a bit, and did wonderful embroideries. At the turn of the century she made an *art nouveau* tapestry for a small room in Friedrichstein, a truly original piece of work. Incidentally, in still another small room there was a tapestry embroidered a hundred and fifty years earlier, in the eighteenth century, by the then mistress of the house. It shows little Chinese figures appliquéd on sackcloth against a background of a painted Oriental landscape.

The occasional visits of the Crown Prince and Crown Princess, or the Crown Princess alone, did not come to an end with the fall of the monarchy; they continued into the 1920s and '30s and were high points in my mother's life. Years later, after the Second World War, when I was a journalist in Hamburg and had written something about some historical event, I learned of a visit by the Empress before the First World War in a letter from a man I did not know personally. His name was Hand, and he was the son of the former chief estate administrator of Friedrichstein. In his letter he said that besides the incident described in my article, another memorable event had taken place on that day—the Empress's visit to Friedrichstein. For weeks, he said, everybody in a position of responsibility in the Königsberg region—the mayors of villages through which the Empress was going to pass, women's clubs, veterans' organizations, schools, and, of course, my mother—was in

Empress Augusta Victoria and my mother in the carriage with our head coachman, Grenda, in front of the castle.

a state of agitation. On the day itself my mother's excitement turned to utter dismay because fifteen minutes before the Empress's scheduled time of arrival my father was nowhere to be found. At that moment, Father, in striking contrast to everyone else's excited air of anticipation, calmly sauntered up to the main door in dirty boots and old trousers. Nevertheless he somehow managed to appear at his post properly attired in the nick of time.

This incident is typical of both my parents: Father, who apparently was always relaxed and in matters of dress fairly casual for his time—"Tell me," a friend once asked him,

*The Empress and my mother, unrecognizable
beneath their enormous hats.*

"who wears your suits when they're new?"—and Mother, who was greatly concerned with appearances and for whom everything had to be *comme il faut.*

On one such occasion I made her very angry when as a teenager I refused to go back to my room and put on more elegant shoes. These protests were my only way of rebelling against what I considered excessive monarchist fuss.

When I was fifteen, I was sent to school at Potsdam and there met Hans Plessen, who was my age. His grandfather had been adjutant general and commandant of the Imperial Headquarters during the First World War, obviously an important personage at court. When we got to know each other better, Hans confided in me—almost like a confession—that he was not a monarchist. I felt very revolutionary when, with deep conviction, I replied, "Neither am I." The Emperor had departed the stage only a few short years before, and considering our backgrounds, such a declaration, if not revolutionary, at least showed that every generation stakes out its own principled positions.

July 12th, my mother's birthday, was always a festive occasion. At morning services, as on all our birthdays, we sang "Praise the Lord," followed by a reading of the 121st Psalm and the hymn "Take My Hands." In the late afternoon the "officials," the inspectors of the estates, would come to offer their congratulations, and cake and wine would be served. In the evening there was a formal dinner, at which, as far back as I can remember until the beginning of the Second World War, three special friends never failed to show up: Adolf von Batocki, Count Manfred Brünneck, and Excellency von Berg.

$\mathcal{T}$HREE FAITHFUL FRIENDS

These three men were as charming as they were interesting. Batocki—as *Oberpräsident* of East Prussia, he was its highest-ranking official—served as Reichs Minister of Agriculture in the First World War; prior to that, at the end of 1914, after the retreat of the Russian army, he had been in charge of the reconstruction of East Prussia's destroyed cities and the resettlement of its refugees. A man of keen intellect, he was imaginative, decisive, and energetic. Being widely respected, he also had no difficulty managing in the chaotic conditions of the immediate postwar era.

Batocki's name has been mentioned in connection with the allegation that East Prussia's big landowners, as opponents of the Weimar Republic's land-reform policy, were responsible for President Hindenburg's ouster of Chancellor Brüning in 1932. This definitely is not true of Batocki, a political supporter of Brüning. He had no part in narrow agrarian machinations, though he may possibly have been looked on with skepticism in Berlin because of his active support of greater self-administration and independence for his home province. His advocacy of greater autonomy for East Prussia had the unqualified support of the people of that province; since East Prussia was cut off from the rest of Germany by the Polish Corridor, it was entirely possible for circumstances to arise demanding prompt on-the-spot decisions. The Corridor was created by what was called the "shameful" Treaty of Versailles. Naturally people never ceased to complain about this.

When we East Prussians went to Berlin we said we were "going to the Reich." We lived not in the Reich but "in the province." Traveling through the Polish Corridor in the early years after 1919 was adventurous. Curtains on train compartments had to be drawn, nobody was allowed to look out, and passengers had to be prepared for any eventuality. It was not unusual for people to be ordered off the train because something in their passports appeared questionable or because they were suspected of having Polish currency on their person.

I remember a story Mother told us when she returned from her first such trip. Apparently a friend of one of her fellow passengers was taken off a train by the Poles for a body search, and they found a message imprinted on her backside. The officials were convinced they'd uncovered a secret agent. It seems that this hapless woman had visited the not very clean toilet on the train and had covered the seat with a newspaper—the print had rubbed off.

The second of our good friends, Count Manfred Brünneck, was a highly cultivated aesthete who dressed in a most idiosyncratic fashion. He would wear a lilac ascot instead of a tie, a yellow jacket, and light-colored spats, which we children called dog blankets because they looked exactly like the funny saddlelike objects that owners put on their little pets to protect them against the cold. Brünneck used snuff, which he carried in a gold case, and blew his nose into a large red handkerchief. He was the *Landeshauptmann* of East Prussia—that is, chief of the provincial administration—a title that seemed very mysterious to me; I never found out what duties it entailed. Many such titles were probably bestowed for reasons of prestige and did not carry with them any specific responsibilities.

Brünneck's property, Bellschwitz, belonged to the district of Neudeck, Hindenburg's estate. It is thus not surprising that Brünneck should have been suspected of having had a hand in Brüning's ouster, although I am convinced that he had as little to do with it as Batocki. Brünneck too was a supporter of Brüning and an opponent of the Home League founded by Kapp, the man behind the reactionary Kapp Putsch of 1920. As a matter of fact, Brünneck had broken with the German National People's Party before 1930.

Immediately after Brüning's ouster, it was said—and there are those who believe it to this day—that the "East Elbe Junkers" had exploited their close ties to Hindenburg to thwart the land reforms instituted by Schlange-Schöningen, commissioner for the eastern provinces. These circles, it was said, had plotted to topple the Brüning cabinet and replace it with a presidential government more receptive to their concerns.

The voluminous correspondence between Brünneck and Brüning in the Secret Archives of Berlin-Dahlem throws some interesting light on this whole matter. On October 12,

1948, Brüning wrote to Brünneck saying he wanted to set the record straight with regard to published tendentious accounts by German émigrés about the role of the German nobility in his ouster: "It was not the nobility that toppled me. . . . On the contrary, in the difficult situations of January and February, 1932, members of the East Prussian and Silesian nobility intervened on my behalf with the Reichs President." In Brüning's opinion, Otto Meissner and General Schleicher were the responsible parties.

Ernst Rudolf Huber writes, in his *Deutsche Verfassungsgeschichte seit 1789 (German Constitutional History Since 1789)*, that it was not "good-neighborly obstructionism" that induced Hindenburg at Neudeck to resist the cabinet's plan for the forced public sale of estates unable to pay their debts, but, rather, the objections of "professional representatives of agriculture," who entertained doubts about it. Hindenburg also believed that auctions held by an arm of the government without its being petitioned to do so by the creditors, in proceedings where the government would also appear as a "buyer" and set the price, constituted expropriation without a legal basis.

Fritz von Berg, the third of these friends, and the most conservative, was a rather frequent visitor at Friedrichstein; he never missed July 12th. Uncle Fritz, born in 1866, was a bachelor. He had studied law, become a member of the East Prussian government, a provincial councilor, and finally *Oberpräsident* of East Prussia.

He was extremely nearsighted, wore glasses with thick lenses, had a resonant voice, and spoke in a strangely disjointed fashion, a mannerism that became pronounced on festive occasions. He would begin to speak, three or four words would tumble out, followed by a pause, then another three or four words and another pause. When I was little, I was fascinated by this and would have loved to speak just like him. If he was present at morning services, I always maneuvered to stand next to him and to say the prayer exactly as he did: "Our Father"—pause—"who art in Heaven"—pause . . .

Everybody treated Uncle Fritz with great respect. After my father's death, Mother would occasionally turn to him for advice or help with a problem. Once he gave his opinion it was usually accepted, despite our ingrained skepticism. He was a moral institution.

When Uncle Fritz came into our lives, his active life was already behind him and he lived reclusively at Markienen, his estate. However, before and during the First World War, as a friend of the Emperor and at times quite an influential one, he had played an important role. He apparently was involved in the intrigues of the Supreme Army Command—in other words, Hindenburg and Ludendorff—that in 1917 led to the overthrow of Chancellor Bethmann Hollweg. A year later he became head of the civilian cabinet, an office encompassing a variety of important functions—editing the Emperor's speeches, having a voice in the staffing of crucial governmental positions on the Presidential and ecclesiastical levels. In the course of time, he found himself more and more often in the position of adviser to the Emperor, which inevitably earned him the charge of having made a poor job of it. He was criticized for intervening in foreign policy, and some circles took a jaundiced view of his old-fashioned Prussianism and his activist Protestantism.

But we were not really aware of the many different hats he wore. We knew Uncle Fritz only as a wonderfully kind man who was involved in public affairs, as someone who, although accustomed to moving among the famous of the world, was also concerned with those closer to home.

One day I ran into him in a shop in Königsberg digging around in helpless myopic confusion among sweaters and knitted hats in search of Christmas presents for the children of his household staff. And my older brother told me about an unforgettable scene he had witnessed during one of his visits to Markienen. A servant had come into the room to announce a visitor, saying, "A man outside wishes to speak to Your Excellency, but he won't say who he is nor what he wants." "Ask him to come in." Thereupon a young man entered and, bowing his head politely, introduced himself. Uncle Fritz peered at him searchingly for a moment, and then said to the man, "Are you his son?" "Yes, Your Excellency." The young man was the son of a soldier who, a good forty years earlier, had served in the First Guards Regiment under Lieutenant von Berg.

HONOR AND PRIVILEGE

My mother was very conscious of her position and her responsibilities, and that consciousness manifested itself in two ways. She was guided by the principle of what one *should* do and, more important, what one should *not* do, and her commitment to these two precepts was rigid and unshakable. When she asserted or objected that something should not be done, it was a verdict that brooked no contradiction. Nothing more remained to be said. And her notion of what one should or should not do was grounded in the rules of a society, a privileged caste, that had evolved over generations. Of course, privileges also brought with them obligations based on a rigidly structured code of behavior. People who failed to live up to that code, who flaunted its rules, were either automatically excluded from society or removed from sight and "shipped off to America."

Convention—a concept future generations were to rebel against so passionately, seeing in it the embodiment of shallowness, superficiality, inanity—was extremely important to my mother and her contemporaries. I believed that what mattered was personal conduct and personal style rather than convention, and I too rebelled against it in my youth. We learn to appreciate its social utility only after we find out that instability inevitably follows when convention is trampled on.

Honor, the legacy of the age of chivalry, lay at the heart of my mother's code. No sacrifice was too great for the honor of serving the king, of bringing honor to the family name, of protecting one's country. In a way, honor was the complementary factor to privilege. One gets nothing for free under any system of government.

Honor meant absolute loyalty to the king and to the prevailing system of values. Serving the ruler, assuring the continuity of that system, was a matter of self-interest, even if the majority of those who served might not recognize the linkage. For the landed aristocracy, the overlapping relationship of property and sovereignty, as well as the nobility's role in the administration from minister to county executive, helped to cement its alliance with the throne. The rules of the game—and this too was important—became a protective shield against all sorts of challenges, a kind of security rail.

Behavior that violated this concept of honor simply was not tolerated. Divorces among officers and high officials were out of the question and meant automatic loss of position. Debt was almost as serious an offense. Officers who could not pay their debts believed that they would have to shoot themselves, and frequently did. These values persisted, regardless of what Schiller had to say in his *Kabale und Liebe* or Goethe in *The Sorrows of Young Werther.* To the very end, this society remained a private, hermetically sealed world confident of the validity of its mores. What the poets were saying was literature. It had nothing to do with reality.

Not only did the landed aristocrats lay no claim to being part of the world of the poets and intellectuals, but they took pride in rejecting it—partly out of snobbery and partly because they did not want to be thought pretentious. One of their group once published an article—in itself a slightly suspect enterprise—and, to make matters worse, entitled it in a kind of highbrow way "Ex oriente lux," a misstep that earned him the sobriquet *Orientluchs* (Eastern lynx).

It might perhaps be fair to say that back then honor played the role money plays today as the most highly prized possession. Since money was not so important as it is nowadays, corruption was also not so widespread. Yet, despite all the social safeguards, scandals were not unknown. Most involved love affairs and adultery, not money. And when a scandal did threaten, the first order of business was to close ranks and make sure that no word about the lapse leaked out beyond the confines of one's own class. I can remember the occasional warning "*pas devant les domestiques*" if rumor of a scandal was mentioned at table.

I said my mother's awareness of her position took two forms. The second was her feeling of responsibility for everything that happened in her immediate sphere. If someone in the village became sick, that person had to be cared for. If it involved a minor illness, Mother herself would visit the patient to lend a hand or bring medicines. If the illness was more severe, a nurse was sent in. Occasionally my older sisters had to help tend elderly villagers. During the First World War, my mother set up a shelter for the blind in the village hall; my two older sisters—aged seventeen and eighteen, respectively—assisted by only one helper, looked after the twelve charges housed there.

One Sunday I was sent to the village to bring some cake to old Altrock, our hog laborer, who had fallen ill. I must have been about ten or eleven. Plate in hand, I stood in front of his door and knocked. No answer. Finally I went in, and my terrified reaction to what I saw has remained with me ever since. I found the old man lying on his bed under an enormous feather comforter, his mouth wide open, his face the color of ancient vellum, and flies buzzing about his head. I knew instinctively that Altrock was dead. I put the plate down on the table and ran home as fast as my feet would carry me. For the next few nights I couldn't sleep; I thought I saw Altrock's ghost standing next to my bed.

Even at an early age, I thought that my mother's conversation was studded with clichés. One day, talking about a very intelligent lady who had held forth about Spengler's *Decline of the West,* Mother stated apodictically that women could not understand Spengler. This irked me, and I decided there and then to read Spengler as soon as I was old enough. I never doubted for a moment that I would understand him. Why should women be any less able to think than men? The fact that some of our female visitors were unable to decipher railroad timetables filled me with shame.

In a way, Mother's profound piety counterbalanced her conventionality. She never questioned the workings of fate, even when that led to highly unconventional situations.

One of my sisters, two years older than I, who suffered from what was called mongoloidism, was mentally impaired. Up to the age of eleven, I shared a room with her. In a time less attuned to God than to Sigmund Freud, such an arrangement would certainly be frowned upon, but I regarded it as a matter of course; moreover, it taught me to accept the blows of fate without rebelling.

When this sister reached adulthood, she was sent to an institution in Bethel, and there she remained until we found out that the Nazis, under the euphemistic guise of euthanasia, were killing off the mentally ill. My oldest brother immediately took off for Bethel and brought her home. It turned out that the head of Bethel was able to protect his patients, so I took her back, and she died there shortly after the end of the war.

I remember how on the eve of the Second World War my cousin Gerti Kanitz made fun of my mother's piety. A talented, intelligent, though somewhat cynical man, he had for a time been Minister of Agriculture in the Weimar Republic. He and I were discussing what Hitler and the Nazis might have in store for us, and he remarked rather sarcastically, "Your mother, after all, has a tested recipe. She'll just go on conducting her evening services." I asked with some asperity, "Do you have a better solution?" Today, as I write this, I am reminded of the story about an earthquake. It seems that a major earthquake had reduced a village to rubble; the survivors were looking at the devastation in despair when a peddler with a tray of merchandise slung around his shoulders appeared, calling out, "Pills against earthquakes, pills against earthquakes!" "Leave us alone with that nonsense!" the angry townspeople shouted. "Do you know of anything better?" he asked. "If so, tell me."

$\mathcal{V}$ISITING
RELATIVES

In my childhood, during the First World War, not many guests came to Friedrichstein, and after my father died, in 1920, the official visits that Otto Hentig spoke of ceased altogether. But a handful of very dear relatives continued to come to see us, above all Aunt Sissi Keyserlingk, my mother's closest friend. A romantic, wonderfully warm person, imaginative and musical, she was the translator of Robert Browning as well as a poet in her own right.

In the early 1920s the first, rather primitive radios made their appearance; I remember my oldest sister riding more than ten miles just to see one of these marvels. The Keyserlingks, in Neustadt, had acquired such a box. When I was taken on a visit to them for the first time, I found Aunt Sissi sitting in front of her receiver in ecstasy and whispering, "Divine music—Wagner." She motioned me to sit down quietly and share her pleasure, but all I, not nearly so imaginative, could hear were blurred sounds drowned out by a noise like rain on a tin roof.

One day I went along on a hunt with my hosts' son, who was quite a bit older than I. He bagged a capercailzie, for which he won great praise back at the house; it was a rare feat. I was flattered and made to feel very important because he told everyone within earshot that I had brought him luck. Aunt Sissi must have wanted to keep my fame alive, for after I got back home she sent me a letter with a little bookmark to commemorate the great event. On the bookmark, somewhat bent out of shape and covered with ink spots, was a picture of a parrot, not a capercailzie, and her message: "We'll simply call the little creature a capercailzie."

Her husband, Uncle Heinrich, was an object of constant wonder. To begin with, he never took off his cap, even indoors, and what was even more startling, he had a kind of tube I had seen nowhere else except with racing horses. It was a silver breathing tube that protruded from his neck in the place where other men wore a collar button. I watched in fascination when he spoke, always expecting the words to come out through the tube instead of his mouth. However, all that ever came out of it were whistling noises and occasionally some spittle.

At the time, a man by the name of Coué, a French pharmacist, was in the news. He advocated autosuggestion as a cure for illness. All one had to do was to repeat a phrase over and over again with deep conviction, and then, according to Coué, hope would turn into reality. Aunt Sissi wrote that Uncle Heinrich was not feeling too well and that she sat at his bedside, repeating over and over again: "Heinrich is feeling much better. . . . Heinrich is feeling much better. . . . But," she wrote, "it didn't do Heinrich any good. Instead, I feel better with each passing day."

One of our rare visitors, and one whom I loved dearly, was Uncle Siegfried Eulenburg. Even as a child I could sense that he was special. For some reason or other he liked me. When greeting me, he held out both his hands to me— a gesture that I had never seen anywhere else and whose warmth won me over completely. Uncle Siegfried was the last commander of the First Guards Regiment (Infantry)— the pride of Prussia since the time of William I. (Inciden-

Siegfried Count zu Eulenburg-Wicken, the last commander of the First Guards Regiment (Infantry).

tally, it was the traditional regiment of the later IR 9, the one that lost most officers in the anti-Hitler resistance.) In the First World War, Siegfried Eulenburg was awarded the Pour le Mérite Order with Oak Leaves—a rare decoration then.

A friend of ours, Kurt Plettenberg, who in the First World War served in Uncle Siegfried's regiment, told me of an incident during the Russian campaign that made a deep impression on me. Kurt and Uncle Siegfried were sitting in a peasant hut somewhere in Russia playing chess. It was a peaceful evening with no enemy fire; suddenly Eulenburg got up, picked up the chessboard carefully, and said to the startled Plettenberg, "Come, let's go to the other side of the house." Half an hour later a grenade destroyed the part of the house they had been sitting in.

In January 1945, when the Russians came and all of us fled, Uncle Siegfried got into his coach with a young helper next to him and his wife in the back, and set out for the West. He was born on October 10, 1870, which meant that he was seventy-five years old when he was forced to leave his home. He rode almost twelve hundred miles to Lake Constance, where his daughter-in-law's parents, State Secretary Ernst von Weizsäcker and his wife, had a house.

When Uncle Siegfried's wife died he picked out the headstone, and next to her name he had his name and date of birth inscribed so that later only the date of his death would have to be added. He did not want to cause other people any more trouble and expense than absolutely necessary.

Another uncle, Carol Lehndorff—famous throughout East Prussia for his bizarre behavior—came to Friedrich-

stein only once during my childhood. He arrived from
Königsberg in a taxi, and continued on in it to his estate,
Steinort, a distance of about a hundred miles. This was
absolutely sensational: taxis were used only in the city, not
for trips in the countryside. The fact that it could be done at
all was beyond belief.

One day Uncle Carol, inspired by one of his extravagant
ideas, invited all the Lehndorff children and me to Steinort.
The only condition he laid down was: no adults. Steinort, a
beautiful, large estate at the edge of a lake, had been in his
family for four hundred years. The house itself was old, not
particularly beautiful, and somewhat neglected; no woman
had been in charge for fifty years, and it had not become
more livable under the aegis of Carol Lehndorff, that strange
bachelor. In my room, which apparently suffered from
permanent dampness, the rotted legs of the wooden bed
had been replaced by bricks, the curtains were moth-eaten,
and the furniture was extremely fragile. When one of us
tried to open a window, it came crashing down—glass,
frame, everything.

Uncle Carol, vastly amused by this visiting band of
teenagers—we ranged in age from thirteen to sixteen—told
us we could do whatever we wanted so long as we were on
time for dinner. Apparently he had a surprise in store for us.
He had indeed prepared something unusual: an eating
contest involving gulls' eggs, with a prize going to the
winner. I no longer remember who won; all I do remember
is that we ate dozens of these green-marbled eggs, followed
by chocolate pudding.

The party was successful beyond our wildest expectations. The next morning, I got out of bed feeling wretched and found most of the others lying in their beds wan and still; next to the youngest stood a large white pail.

Uncle Carol's dining room was generally a hive of activity, not only at the time of that particular visit. In the summer Steinort would be filled with people, for Uncle Carol was in the habit of inviting whomever he happened to run into and took a liking to. And come they did, bag and baggage, and stayed, sometimes for weeks. Most of the time Uncle Carol couldn't even remember who these people were, and when things got too lively for him he retreated to his private quarters. The young people were occasionally permitted to visit him in his two small, darkened rooms. My cousin Hans Lehndorff has described these visits:

> Most of the time he lay in bed, pince-nez on his nose, reading or studying coins and coin catalogues. The cabinet one had to squeeze by to get to his bed contained about two hundred and eighty thousand specimens, probably the largest Prussian coin collection of his day. In the course of assembling it he had also become an expert in the field. He corresponded with numismatists and almost always had one or more as guests for weeks or months at a time.

As a young man, Carol Lehndorff had led a rather wild life; he was a spendthrift, got into debt, traveled all over the world, and generally caused his family a great deal of worry. Stories about him continued to be told even in his later years. On the occasion of the fall harvest festival of 1933, when his workers came to the manor house to present the harvest crown, he stood on the balcony to make his little speech. He supposed he should end it with the salutation appropriate to that time. He began, then paused and, looking around perplexedly, said, "Confound it all, what's the name of that fellow?" Remembering that the salutation had something with "Heil!" he finally ended with, "Well, then, *Waidmannsheil* [good hunting]!"

In his book *Menschen, Pferde, weites Land (People, Horses, Countryside),* Hans Lehndorff tells a wonderful story about Carol when he was doing his military service in a small Pomeranian garrison under the command of a reputed martinet, who, so Carol's mother hoped, would manage to drum some sense into her unpredictable wastrel son. On his Sundays off, Carol was fond of attending the races at Karlshorst, near Berlin. There he met with his friends and occasionally himself rode. His commander also enjoyed the races, but he would leave immediately after the main event to catch the last train back to the garrison. He could not understand how Carol managed to stay till the end and still report for duty punctually at six the next morning. It was simple: Carol took a night freight train going in the desired direction. The only hitch was that passengers were not allowed on the train unless they were escorting animals. To legitimize his presence, Carol had his orderly bring a sheep to the train.

When the commander finally figured out the causal connection between the unprecedented accumulation of sheep in the company's stable and Carol's punctuality, he decided to change the company schedule. The freight train arrived at the garrison station at 5:30 a.m. and reveille was at six. The commander now moved it up to 5:30. To his utter astonishment, the scenario at Karlshorst remained unchanged: the commander left and the lieutenant stayed, making no move to leave the track early. One Sunday the commander was held up on his way to the station and missed the last train. He turned to the stationmaster for help. "You're out of luck," the stationmaster told him. "As a rule, a lieutenant with a sheep in tow takes the freight train, and you could have joined him, but that train doesn't get to your stop until five-thirty." After some thought he added, "Tonight the lieutenant ordered a special train around midnight. If you ask him, I'm sure he'll take you along."

PROHIBITIONS AND TRANSGRESSIONS

We children—at least we three youngest ones—saw our parents only rarely: they lived downstairs; we lived upstairs with our governess, where we ate together and played together. In the evening Mother would come up to hear our prayers; when there were guests, we had to go down to say good night.

In retrospect I must confess that I did not learn anything important either from my parents or from the governesses that kept coming and going. Whatever I did learn, I absorbed from the general atmosphere of our household and from the people we grew up among. For naturally we would escape from the clutches of our official caretakers whenever possible and run off to the carpentry, the stables, or the garden nursery, all of them far more interesting than the castle itself. The hothouse was a favorite haunt during the grape season. It was kept under lock and key, but we were accomplished break-in artists. I still have a scar on my leg dating back to the time when I was chosen to crawl through a small window whose glass we had broken but that still had shards and splinters on the frame.

We did not have to be instructed to own up to misdeeds if we were guilty. Our sense of responsibility grew out of our sense of community. The village children were our playmates; besides, the workmen didn't treat us with kid gloves and had no compunction about blaming us for broken windowpanes or missing tools. Tattling or blaming others would have violated our sense of honor and fairness. We did it, and that's all there was to it. And since one of us was usually among the ringleaders, taking the blame was natural.

Tolerating pain without complaining was also part of our honor code. To whine if you happened to hurt yourself climbing a tree or in a game was contemptible. I remember a time when my four older siblings beat their legs with willow twigs to see which one would be the first to cry out. The enterprise was aborted for lack of results. If no one gave in, it was no fun.

Most of our accidents happened on horseback. Broken arms or legs were commonplace. Once, two of us were in the hospital in Königsberg at the same time; my sister Yvonne with a fractured vertebra, my brother Dieter with a broken thighbone.

One day while out riding with my oldest brother—our horses were rather immature and unpredictable—I came to a ditch, and my mare leaped across and threw me over her head. I lay on the ground, but fortunately I had held on to the reins. We were a long way from home and my arm hurt mightily. "Never mind," said my brother. "Get back on the horse or we'll be late." He was convinced that my arm couldn't be broken; it didn't hurt enough for that. And so I pulled myself back up on the horse and felt a searing pain, followed by a soft clicking sound. In view of the convincing brotherly diagnosis I had little choice but to keep going. When we got home, the village nurse was summoned to massage the arm. But by next morning the pain was intolerable and I was sent to Königsberg where the arm was X-rayed. The diagnosis: both bones of my arm, the thick and the thin, were fractured. According to the doctor, the thin one probably broke when I got back up on the horse.

On the whole, rules at home were strictly enforced. Many things—more than one might expect—were forbidden. Yet in that respect ours was a happy childhood, for these prohibitions offered the only avenue of transgression we had open to us—namely, ignoring them. Nothing gave us greater pleasure than violating taboos.

Occasionally my older brothers or sisters were punished for breaking a rule and forbidden to ride for a few days; they circumvented this restriction by going riding at night, "before dew and daylight." They had an arrangement with the night watchman: at four in the morning he would tug at a long string, the other end of which was attached to the pillow of one of the sleeping conspirators, who then woke up the rest, and they crept out and saddled their horses. By six, all of them would be back in bed, waiting to be awakened at their usual time, seven o'clock.

We little ones were allowed to shoot sparrows with air guns, but under no circumstances were we permitted to go out armed with a rifle or shotgun without adult supervision. Once, on a visit with our Lehndorff cousins, to the Dohnas at Waldburg — it was March and still very cold — we saw a flight of wild geese overhead, which electrified us, first because a wild-goose hunt was the most exciting of all hunts, and also because there were no adults around. So we ran over to the big gun cabinet, took out some guns, and

My older brothers and sisters, Christoph bringing up the rear, playing war games with the village children during the First World War.

loaded them with the heaviest shot, powerful enough to fell a roebuck or a wild boar. Lighter ammunition, like that used to hunt partridges, would simply have ricocheted off the oily feathers of wild geese.

The elder Dohna and Lehndorff boys (we were all between the ages of twelve and fifteen) had taken the best guns, and all that was left for me was an old rifle of a kind I had never used. We fanned out over the marshes, in the hope that the geese would decide to settle there for the night. My companion was the youngest of the Dohna cousins, the unarmed twelve-year-old Konstantin. We waited, our legs half submerged in the icy water. Nothing moved. It got darker and darker, and we decided to return home.

On the way back we came to a broad ditch spanned by a

Head coachman Grenda with my four older brothers and sisters.

makeshift bridge—just two rods, not even planks. As we were getting ready to cross the ditch, I heard the honking of approaching geese. With frozen fingers I cocked the gun and scanned the dark sky, but could see nothing. We stopped briefly, and then Konstantin went ahead so that I could hand him the gun to keep it from falling into the water. I held it out toward him, stock first, the barrel pointing toward me. No sooner had he touched the weapon than there was a powerful noise like a thunderbolt and I fell backward. A forest ranger rushed over to us and said to Konstantin, "Well, now you've shot her dead." Oh God, I said to myself, now I'm dead, and no wonder, considering the heavy shot. As it turned out, the bullet had missed me by millimeters. Only the right side of my jacket was a little singed. Somewhat the worse for wear, the two of us trotted back home.

I did not see my older brothers and sisters much more frequently than I saw my parents. They were generally busy with other things. When they caught sight of me, they had me run errands for them, but I didn't really mind because it made me feel important. I think I learned a lot from them and the way they dealt with me. Despite their undemonstrative demeanor, they were extremely considerate if something happened to me—or, for that matter, to anyone. They were imaginative and witty, and I never heard them tell an off-color, let alone an obscene story. And something else about them struck me only much later: unlike so many people, they never talked about themselves. On the contrary, they were very discreet about their personal affairs, and downright secretive about the affairs of others.

$\mathcal{M}$Y REAL TEACHERS

In thinking back on my childhood what I remember most of all is the feeling of being part of a community in which we children had a definite place, something like the ball bearings between two levels, the top and the bottom. When I was confirmed, which most people seem to equate with "entering upon life," Grenda said to my mother, "Well, Excellency, now we've got all of them through, and I think we can be quite pleased."

I would like to mention in particular Grenda and some of the other exceptional personalities in our immediate circle, and the role they played in my development. Grenda was called "boss" both by the stable hands and by us children. He was an unquestioned authority figure—at any rate, he ruled quite autocratically—and none of us ever questioned his claim to authority. He must have been a sergeant in the army, and he considered the military the only reliable educational institution. "What they need is the army, that will make human beings out of them," he used to say about his stableboys, and in its place he offered what he considered essential basic training. Nor did he treat us very differently. If for some reason or other he was displeased by something we had done, or if he just wanted to demonstrate his power, he would lay down the law: "No riding today. Yesterday the bunch of you went so fast that the black horse got sweaty and now he's coughing." "Well, then, how about the chestnut?" "The chestnut is lame, he can't go today either." Fortunately the boss had a weakness: fine cigars. If we wanted to make sure of his good will we would steal some cigars at the house and bring them to him. It worked like a charm. Another thing we could rely on was that Grenda would take our side. If he saw a tutor or a governess looking for us because we were supposed to be doing our homework, he would lock us in the harness room and swear by all that was holy that there was nobody in his stable.

The harness room, incidentally, was like a jewel box. It smelled of freshly waxed leather, and the buckles gleamed with the brilliance of polished silver. On Sundays the stable for the saddle and carriage horses (the workhorses were kept in the yard) was a joy to behold, with the two stalls for ponies, two for mares and foals, and eight for the other saddle horses symbolically locked by white crisscrossed straps, with straw mats interwoven in red cord placed before each of them.

Grooming the horses was our great passion. It wasn't easy: arms outstretched, we would swing the horse brushes with a sweeping motion and, in that same motion, scrape them against the curry comb. The really difficult work was sweeping the dust, which had to go into twelve five-inch strips, one in front of each stall where the straw mats were put on Sunday. The chief said that was how it had to be done if we wanted to be taken seriously.

I learned a great deal from our staff. The chauffeur showed me how to take a carburetor apart, and in the carpentry shop I learned about planing and joining. I suppose I was eager to prove that we in the castle were every bit as competent as anybody else. The countrypeople seemed to be able to do a little bit of everything: masonry, carpentry, plumbing. One of our great favorites was our carpenter, Master Klein. He taught my brothers how to work with wood until finally they were even able to make window frames. I, being too little, was not allowed to touch the

The entire domestic staff—footmen, coachmen, housemaids—lined up in anticipation of a visit by the Empress. In front, my four older brothers and sisters, and in the rear Master Klein, a favorite member of our household.

mechanical drill, but I was allowed to plane simple boards. When Master Klein grew too old to handle the heavy wood, he was given a special job: every morning he had to wind the grandfather clocks in all the rooms of the castle.

In a house as big as Friedrichstein many details had to be attended to, and those who had proved their reliability and trustworthiness were given various of these chores. Thus it was Weber's job to keep the fireplaces stocked with wood, which he carried in a big basket slung across his back. When I was a child we did not have central heating; every room had its own stove and fireplace. I shall never forget Weber's heavy footsteps on the staircase, the first sound I heard on awakening.

Weber's wife was in charge of the laundry. Every two weeks a vast quantity of laundry would be brought down to the pond to be washed and then hung up to dry in a huge shed. This job involved the additional help of six to eight women from the village who, chattering away, washed the sheets and towels in enormous vats. The next step in this process took place in the house itself. There, in the ironing room, stood a huge mangle apparatus, weighted down by rocks and set in motion by a big flywheel. I was permitted to operate it occasionally as the rollers glided back and forth over the sheets, pressing them. The girls who taught me to iron accompanied their work with songs that could be heard in the rooms below. Sentimental folk songs were my favorites. Most of the time the girls were on the side of us children; if we were punished and sent to bed without supper, we were likely to find a plate of sandwiches on the night table. I don't know whether their gesture was a

symbol of the solidarity of the underprivileged and op-
pressed or merely the normal unity of the young against the
old.

It must have been in the beginning of the 1920s when
two lamps brought the first electric light into the castle. One
of them illuminated the staircase, the other the room where
we gathered in the evening to read. This major innovation
was made possible by a generator installed in the old mill
about three hundred feet from the house.

When I think back to the most important persons of my
youth, three more people stand out, one of whom I feared
and the other two I held in high regard. The one I feared was
Quednau, my mother's personal maid. She was a tattletale, I
suppose because she wanted to worm her way into my
mother's confidence. My mother called her "Quedchen,"
but the rest of us called her "Quecke," after a particularly
noxious weed. Once she got a boil on her mouth that had to
be lanced, which prompted Grenda, who could not bear
her, to proclaim that it was obvious that people are punished where they have sinned. She was an accomplished
seamstress, and when my older sisters outgrew the dresses
she made for them they were handed down to me.

The skills of Fritz, our butler, a sober, extremely proper
man and a highly esteemed member of the household, were
not limited to his specific duties. He could do many things,
from repairs to growing melons. Eventually he was con-
scripted into the people's militia, and to our deep sorrow he
did not make it back from the war. On all East Prussian
estates, the relationship to the butler was traditionally close
and warm. When Albert died, the Lehndorffs' butler whom

we children loved because he was always so jolly, it was taken for granted that I would travel to Preyl to attend his funeral.

If Fritz reprimanded us for violating the house rule about wearing muddy boots indoors, we obeyed him because we knew that failure to take them off meant more work for him. Once he had mentioned it, we left our dirty shoes in the vestibule, like the villagers who left their wooden clogs at the door when they came to petition our parents. The things we learned from the household staff and workers made a far more lasting impression on us than the instruction of people officially in charge of our education.

Fritz knew everything and was interested in everything. One day he explained to me that a particular rug about to be repaired was not a kilim, as I had claimed, but a bokhara. "Who said so?" "The book by Hasenbalg, and the Count told me that's the best book about rugs. There it is." And he pointed to a big volume on the bookshelf. I had never noticed it.

Fritz's interest in carpets had its reasons. In addition to the lovely eighteenth-century Flemish tapestries woven especially for two of our rooms, there were the carpets that my father had been collecting over the years. In the winter it was fantastic to see rugs of all sizes spread out on the huge snow-covered lawn in front of the castle and an army of maids and villagers swinging carpet beaters in unison. According to Father, this was the only proper way to clean rugs; rough brushes, which were likely to damage them, were strictly forbidden. Until the next snowfall the lawn remained a patterned spread of rectangles and squares, some light, some dark, depending on the amount of dust in each rug.

Krebs, our head gardener, was an unforgettable personage: big-bellied, mustachioed, a giant of a man who walked with a cane, always wore a straw hat, and headed an army of assistants. His unshakable serenity was confidence-inspiring, which was probably why he was the one to be called to the castle at the first hint of a thunderstorm: Mother was afraid of lightning. We would all sit around in our red flannel dressing-gowns and wait for the big moment when Krebschen would arrive and tell us stories about long ago. We were fascinated by Krebs for still another reason: he had a huge eagle owl that he took on crow hunts, and occasionally he would take one of us children along too. We would start out at dawn with the owl chained to a perch on

This was the view from the balcony of Friedrichstein.

a little platform atop a six-foot pole, a construction he called "Jule." Then we would hide in the bushes, waiting—frequently in vain. However, now and then crows and sometimes other birds were lured by the owl on the pole. To protect his valuable owl from harm, Krebs would shoot at these birds while they were still at a safe distance, and if he hit one the owl was assured of its next meal.

Krebs was in charge of the orangerie, which in winter housed the citrus trees in big tubs. Once it got warm, they were moved outdoors to the front of the castle. He was also in charge of the garden, the hothouse for the grapes, and a huge vegetable garden with numerous hotbeds. Self-sufficiency was the rule in country households. Nothing was bought; everything—eggs, vegetables, fruit—was home-grown, and consumed when it was ripe. Thus for weeks we would eat spinach, followed by peas until they grew to the size of cannonballs, then carrots. In addition, everything was canned or otherwise preserved for the winter: carrots were buried in sand, gherkins were put up in stone jugs each covered by a wooden lid weighted down by a rock. Nor was meat ever bought. Fall and winter were the seasons for game, and of course there was mutton and veal all year round, and everything the chicken coop had to offer. If a product turned out to be especially good and big, everyone, owner and help alike, glowed with pride. Once a rather good artist was commissioned to paint one particular grape before it was presented to the Empress. Why? Because, according to the inscription on the painting, it had reached extraordinary proportions: it weighed eleven pounds. And one of the fishermen once caught a forty-pound pike, which was served on an ironing board to show off its imposing size.

$\mathscr{S}$ELF-SUFFICIENCY

The ultimate in self-sufficiency was the semiannual hog-butchering, which guaranteed an adequate supply of hams and sausages for months to come. It was an event that everyone, especially the kitchen staff, looked forward to — the village women were called in to help, and there was brandy and much merrymaking. No statesman could take greater pride in negotiating a treaty than did Mamsellchen, the cook, as she surveyed the jars of preserved meats and the racks of ham that testified to a hard week's work.

Mushroom-gathering and raspberry-picking expeditions were yet other examples of self-sufficiency. Early in the morning we would set forth in a long open cart whose floor was covered with two rows of straw pads, seating for the pickers — the house and kitchen maids and we children. Two placid, patient horses were harnessed, because these excursions were likely to take some hours. On setting out we would sing folk songs. In those days, before canned music, people sang much more than they do nowadays, mostly in the morning on the way to the fields; on the way back they were generally too tired. Among my earliest and loveliest memories are the sad, melancholic folk songs of the Russian prisoners of war who worked on the farm in the First World War.

We loved these expeditions to the woods to pick raspberries or to gather the small round caps of fresh mushrooms that carpeted the lush Pregel meadows. We'd compete over who could pick the most, and by the end of the day the big potato baskets we had brought would be full. Back at the house the mushrooms were cut up, then dried for the winter, either in a special oven also used to dry fruit or simply strung up on cords.

I remember my unhappiness when my brother, upon taking over the estate, changed from self-supply to a market economy. He said it made no sense to produce things ourselves that could be bought more cheaply from others—like eggs and chickens. Predictably one day the vegetable garden was going to fall victim to the same sort of argument. I found these changes dismaying, even though I knew that my brother was right, but it meant saying goodbye to a unique aspect of our world.

Winter ice-making was another tradition that, to my sorrow, had to be abandoned. Before the invention of refrigeration, the storage of meats and other perishables was a problem solved, on every well-run estate, by an ice cellar, generally in the garden under a shade tree. Ours was a three-foot-deep dugout with a straw roof—straw was better insulation than slates—and packed-dirt walls. In it was stored enough ice in winter to see us through the following summer. When the ice on the lake got to be about a foot deep, our manager detailed eight or ten of the farmhands to ice-making. They would go down to the frozen lake carrying saws and long poles with hooks, cut huge rectangular blocks out of the ice, and fish them from the water with their poles. Then they cut the blocks into smaller pieces and brought them to the ice cellar on sleds. This procedure, which might take an entire day, usually turned into something of a party, for to keep the workers warm and happy vast quantities of grog were served and consumed.

While all this was going on, the village children amused themselves in their own fashion. The boys would hammer a post into the ice and connect it to a long pole, which they rotated around the post. It operated on the principle of a compass, with one leg firmly positioned and the other turning concentrically around it. The children then attached a sled to the end of the pole by ropes and set it in motion: the rotational speed of the pole made for a wild centrifugal carousel. This game usually ended with bruises and an occasional concussion.

Children can be remarkably inventive if there is nothing for them to buy. We taught ourselves how to swim by making floats out of thick reed pads which we tied together with string. Those lucky enough to get hold of two pig bladders used the same method. We made fifes out of willow twigs the thickness of a thumb by cutting off a twig about eight inches long, tapping it with our penknives until the bark was separated and the reed could be extracted. Out of this we carved a mouthpiece, cut a notch into the bark, and then pushed the shortened reed back into the bark. Particularly skillful carvers even could make flutes in this way.

As I grew up, I felt very torn: on the one hand I mourned the passage of the old ways; and, on the other, the changes in the world could not come quickly enough for me. Once, as a teenager, I asserted that it would be good if the Ottenhagen estate, which was part of Friedrichstein, were to be broken up and distributed to new settlers. Mother, who was certainly not without social awareness and was involved in various charitable activities, was irked by my disloyal recommendation and told me not to utter such nonsense. I refrained from any further discussion, thinking that the old generation just had different ideas and it was best to leave matters alone.

Hog-butchering and ice-making were welcome diversions, but the most important and popular event was the harvest festival. A real orchestra would come to play dance music throughout the night—waltzes and polkas for old and young. The loudest applause greeted the grannies from the village when they got up to dance. As long as Mother was alive she would open the harvest dance partnered by the estate foreman. They would dance a few rounds by themselves while the others stood on the sidelines, looking on and clapping. After Mother's death, my oldest brother took over this role, which made things more interesting, because he would open the dance with one of the local girls. The question of which one he would choose naturally occupied everybody for weeks before the big day.

Long before the festival a crown of grain spikes—the

harvest crown—was brought to the castle. This was one of a number of old rituals having to do with grain. The first stalks of the new crop were always mowed by hand, and then my oldest brother had to come to the field, where the laborers would tie a few spikes around his arm, thus symbolically taking him hostage; he had to buy his freedom, and the substantial ransom he paid went toward the purchase of beer and spirits. As a child I liked to go along to the fields and listen to the strangely mystical sayings recited at these rites.

In my childhood grain was still harvested by a very simple horse-drawn contraption. By the time I was an adult, we were using combines, and my brother and I were deter-

A sight rarely seen in the modern age of combines:
stacked sheaves of grain drying in the field.

mined to turn Friedrichstein into a modern, efficient enterprise. Under the guidance of Professor Gerhard Preusschen we charted production costs and other expenditures, and we bought every laborsaving device modern technology had to offer: threshers, tractors, even pneumatic blowers for the silo. Yet long before 1939, with every new piece of machinery we bought or every new house we built for the workers, we'd say, "The Russians are going to enjoy this." There was no doubt in our minds that the madman who was ruling Germany would get us into a war and that the Russians would be the ultimate beneficiaries.

I remember in particular a harvest festival at Quittainen, one of the family properties. My brother delivered the traditional speech and by custom the foreman was supposed to respond. To everyone's surprise, however, it was the handyman, Marx, who rose to speak. I will never forget what he said to my brother: "Count, if someone has to go on one of those Strength Through Joy trips again, then, please, not I." Strength Through Joy, a Nazi recreational program designed to demonstrate a sense of community and social concern, sponsored vacations for select, deserving individuals—in this instance, a two-week stay in Mallorca. After giving the matter a great deal of thought, Chief Inspector Klatt had recommended Marx, his best, most reliable worker, even though he could not really spare him. Hearing the lucky winner's devastating comment, Klatt said, "Marx is absolutely right. Next time we'll send Schwarz, he's not much use anyway."

$\mathcal{T}$HE CHANGELESS RHYTHM
OF THE SEASONS

When I was little, many of the things that are now part of everyday life were not yet known. We had neither radio nor television, and cars were a rarity. If by chance a car found its way onto an East Prussian country road, horses were likely to shy or bolt. I once saw a peasant jump off his cart, take off his jacket, and drape it over the head of his horse to shield it from the sight of one of those infernal machines. "Diversions" in the real meaning of the word did not exist, and so we were able to devote ourselves to people, to nature, to animals—above all to our horses, dogs, and rabbits.

The changeless rhythm of the seasons dictated the rhythm of our lives, and memories of the seasons are deeply etched in my mind. Spring, when the lakes and streams turned blue and the reeds golden yellow, brought release from a long winter. Then the wind would shake the old trees and the earth would tremble and make us feel strangely apprehensive. The crows began returning to fields about to regain their color, and soon lapwings would come, followed by starlings and storks. The woods smelled of spring, and in the morning sun the pale early green of the beeches shone against the stately dark firs. We knew then that winter, the long wait for the resurgent heartbeat of nature, was finally over.

In East Prussia it took but a few days for the seemingly endless winter to be transformed into the shining splendor of spring. Now the village children took twice as long to walk to school, for splashing in puddles of stagnant water in the deep ruts of the country roads was such fun. The farmers set about readying their rusted machinery, and in the evening they stood in their doorways and dreamily contemplated the newly planted beds and the first buds on the shrubs of their gardens. Before long the broken shells of blue-tinged starling eggs were found on the ground, and the

Springtime at a fish hatchery on what was called "Wild Lake," in the Pregel Valley. In East Prussia the endless winter turned into luminous spring almost overnight.

ceaseless chirping of fledglings filled the air. Marsh mar-
igolds bloomed along the roadside, purplish meadow cab-
bage peeked out from the tall pasture grass bending
majestically under the scythe before sinking down in long,
orderly rows.

The days passed quickly and in summer the nights were
short. No sooner had the sky turned dark in the west than
the rising sun in the east was reflected in the morning dew.
And who could ever forget the coming harvest, the gentle
breezes sweeping over the fields of ripening silvery awns of
grain? Then, during a few hot days in July, the reapers,
rumbling monotonously, cut broad swaths, making their

A summer afternoon.

way through the tall, dense, yellow growth. Later, back on the farm could be heard the melancholy hum of the threshing machines and, in the stables, redolent with the odor of sweating horses, the snap of the whip urging them back to the fields for another load of grain.

The best time of year came after the harvest was in and the fields had turned into vast expanses of stubble made for riding, preferably on a chestnut from the Trakehnen stud. Those who have never experienced the rapture of unrestrained freedom and weightlessness in the saddle have missed one of the great sensations life has to offer: with the world, clothed in a thousand colors and filled with heavenly

Autumn, when heavy rains caused the Pregel River to overflow and wild geese stopped over on their journey to the south, ushered in the most exciting hunts of the year.

scents, at your feet, as beautiful and unspoiled as on the
First Day, the only sounds the rhythmic snorting and hoofbeats of the horse and the soft creaking of the leather
harness, and every now and then a cool breeze as one passes
under the shade of an old oak tree.

Bright red rowanberries glow against the pale blue autumnal sky. With each passing day, the golden leaves of the
birches grow more luminous, the pastures take on the look
of old worn velvet, the elks in the brush become more
reclusive, and huge flocks of migratory birds set out for the
south. The storks and starlings and all the smaller birds
leave long before the majestic swans and cranes and wild

*The deep East Prussian winter in the park of Friedrichstein. There
were months of below-freezing cold, and snow blanketed the land
from December to March.*

geese depart, strung out like pearls across the reddish evening sky, taking life and joy with them.

This marked the beginning of the melancholy, rainy dark season. Every day the roads became more impassable. Carts made their way over the sodden beet fields with difficulty, and leaves whirled in the wind along the tree-lined roads. By November we began lighting our lamps in midafternoon and making fires to warm our frozen feet and hands. Only preparations for Christmas managed to stir people from their lethargy. The village children would offer suggestions for decorating the Nativity scene in the community house. Countless batches of stollen and pfeffernüsse were baked for the village Christmas festivities; here and there the traditional rider on a white horse would turn up, and the monotonous sound of his bass fiddle intermingled with the shrieks of girls frightened by the legendary figures of bear, stork, and rider.

After that came the time for books. By the age of fifteen, I had read everything on our shelves: Thomas Mann, Knut Hamsun, Stefan Zweig, Franz Werfel, Leonhard Frank, Hans Fallada, and of course Hugo von Hofmannsthal and Rainer Maria Rilke and much Dostoevsky.

However, no writer, no poet, could rival the lyricism of our autumnal predawn hunts, when the rising sun turned the dew in the meadows into glittering diamonds, with the lake in the distance shimmering through the trees. The overwhelming beauty and profound silence of such match-less mornings, this miracle of creation, with no living being in sight except for an occasional bumblebee, bird, or doe — these are indissoluble bonds to nature. The gun on the shoulder is nothing but a prop: not a shot must disturb this profound calm. All one's senses and perceptions are sharpened. Everything suddenly becomes clear, life and the universe hold no secrets, and one is suffused by a feeling of boundless gratitude for being allowed to call this place home.

Equally exciting were the excursions with my cousin Sissi Lehndorff, when the two of us, riding with shortened stirrups, would give our horses free rein. Nothing but hoofbeats on the sandy roads and the wind in our hair. We felt indescribably happy, and yet we were filled with the vague premonition that out there, beyond the blue horizon, life would begin in earnest.

Not quite so serene were the spirited traditional hare hunts between Christmas and New Year. Cousins and friends would arrive the evening before the hunt, and by morning things became very lively indeed. After scrambling for cartridges, guns, and fur hats, we'd have a hearty breakfast, climb on our carts, and off we'd go. The snow-covered woods were glorious. The hunters would assemble on the wide paths, about three hundred feet apart, that led to the various blinds; they fanned out among them. And then the long wait began.

Finally we would hear the horn of the hunt master, his instructions echoing through the stillness of the forest: "left flank stay back," "right flank advance." Then gradually the beaters came closer, shouting "hepp, hepp!" and from time to time striking trees with their canes. Things became exciting if a fox was spotted in the distance; peering right and left, he would dart off into a thicket to make his escape.

At noon we would warm ourselves around a fire in a clearing and eat hot pea soup. The hunters, perched on their shooting sticks or on tree stumps, talked about the exciting game they had spotted, and after a brief rest the hunt resumed. A roundup in the open fields, almost like a general staff exercise, frequently ended these hunts. In scenes reminiscent of those on Asian prints, the hunters would form an enormous circle and begin moving from the periphery toward the center, with two or three beaters and then a hunter and more beaters making a slowly advancing chain, driving the hare caught in this fatal encirclement toward the center.

In the evening there was a dinner which we children were also allowed to attend, sitting at our own little table. We had a marvelous time. These evening dinners were our only entertainments. Special children's parties or lavish birthday parties were unheard of; children were not given any special treats. Our parents expected us to grow up and behave properly, and after that one would see what was what. Occasionally we talked about how we would treat *our* children.

Actually we were glad that little attention was paid us; we were content to be left to our own devices. And we were always planning something or other; entertainments arranged by adults would have been a nuisance. When visiting relatives or friends brought their children, we couldn't wait for them to leave; most of the time they were useless as far as we were concerned—either too refined or too timid.

Speaking of being too refined, I must have looked rather messy on occasion, for Grenda would shake his head and say, "And that's supposed to be a little countess?" One day when I was about thirteen, we were expecting a new teacher for me and I was told to wash and put on a decent dress before I went to meet her at the door. Since I was in the midst of cleaning out the rabbit hutch, I lost track of the time and had to rush back to greet her and show her to her room. Having done so, I then washed and changed — *comme il faut,* as my mother liked to say — and went to escort my new teacher to dinner. "Are you Marion?" she asked. I answered yes, I was, whereupon she said somewhat reproachfully, "I thought that you would have come to greet me." After considering for a second whether or not to set her straight, I decided that her erroneous assumption was the lesser of two evils, and kept silent.

$\mathscr{S}$TEINORT:
"THE GREAT WILDERNESS ON THE LAKE"

The Lehndorffs of Steinort were our closest relatives.

Beyond a doubt, theirs was the loveliest estate in all of East Prussia. The manor house, which Marie-Eleonore Dönhoff, Ahasverus Lehndorff's widow, had built after his death in 1688, was not especially noteworthy, for over the years additions were made that played havoc with the original design, but its setting was incomparable.

Jutting into Lake Mauer, the largest in the chain of Masurian lakes, Steinort with its surrounding woods and substantial farms formed a sort of peninsula. The park, with its three-hundred-year-old oaks, stretched down to the lake. I remember an inscribed tablet on one of those ancient trees, dating back to the eighteenth century, on which the proprietor, in medieval French, pledged his loyalty to a friend.

The park at Steinort was renowned for its 300-year-old oaks.
Steinort had been in the possession of the Lehndorff family
since the sixteenth century.

Steinort was a legendary place. Not only was it haunted, like any East Prussian castle worthy of its name, but the lake and the eerie stories it gave rise to, as well as the solitude of its woods and its natural beauty, lent the happy days we spent there an almost magical aura.

Of course the lake itself, a refuge for waterfowl and other species of birds, was one of Steinort's major attractions. There were thousands of ducks and coots, bitterns and cormorants, wild geese and swans, even an occasional osprey. During Steinort's famous July duck hunt, which began on a Saturday and ended the following Monday, between six hundred and seven hundred ducks were likely to be bagged. The beaters, in hip boots, would wade through the reeds and drive the ducks toward the hunters who, standing in wobbly boats, quite often missed their mark.

In winter, when the lake was frozen, it was possible to cross over on the ice to Angerburg, a shortcut of about four miles, though this was not altogether risk-free, as there was a place where each year, when the weather got warmer, the ice would burst and ruts would form. After dark it was always dangerous to cross the lake, and this probably contributed to its air of mystery.

During our childhood, a new sport, ice-sailing, was introduced. A tall sail affixed to a flat, broad sled carried intrepid sailors over the frozen lake at high speeds while they kept a watchful eye for ruts in the ice. Over the years this sport underwent a number of refinements until finally ice-sailing regattas were regularly held on Lake Mauer.

The Lehndorffs had come to East Prussia with the Teutonic Knights. In the early sixteenth century the Order gave Steinort to the family: the deed to "The Great Wilderness on the Lake" is made out to Fabian, Caspar, and Sebastian von Lehndorf. The oaks in the park of Steinort were planted by their heir, Meinhard, born in 1590.

At the age of nineteen Meinhard's son Ahasverus and his nineteen-year-old cousin Eulenburg, accompanied by a tutor, embarked on the Grand Cavalier Tour, a journey that was part of the education of the sons of great houses. The two young men traveled throughout Europe for years, studied military strategy in France and jurisprudence in Bologna, were guests of Cromwell in England, and saw Louis XIV in Paris. Everywhere they went they met other young people from all over the world, like them in quest of knowledge and a broader worldview, and everywhere they were entertained in the homes of notables. In Paris, Ahasverus Lehndorff was received by Queen Christina of Sweden, daughter of Gustavus Adolphus. My cousin Hans Lehndorff has written an account of his ancestor's seven-year journey: "Later, from Italy, he visited the Maltese on their island, made friends with many Knights of the Maltese Order, and was taken along by them on their voyages against Turks and pirates. He was honored by being allowed to be the first to leap onto a pirate vessel, where he learned that the entire crew had either come down with or died of the plague."

This journey of enlightenment was not exactly a pleasure trip; the young men had to follow a highly disciplined routine and adhere to a rigid curriculum. Moreover, travel in those days was both onerous and dangerous. The travelers were attacked by brigands, their carriage frequently broke down on the poor roads, food was often meager—at times nonexistent. A journey such as theirs was bound to be costly even if extreme economy was practiced; consequently even those who could afford it undertook to go only if the investment promised to be worthwhile.

When Ahasverus Lehndorff returned home at the age of twenty-six, the knowledge he had amassed won him universal respect. He went to Poland, where King Kasimir put him in command of all Germans serving in Poland. After six years in Poland he joined the administration of Brandenburg-Prussia, where he held a number of high positions. When Ahasverus died, the Great Elector is alleged to have said: "I have lost my best statesman." In 1686, two years before his death, Emperor Leopold made him a count. That same year Ahasverus married his third wife, Marie-Eleonore Dönhoff. His first two wives had died young.

The family history tells many stories of such early deaths: "His wife, who died at twenty-eight, was the mother of eight children," or, "She died at twenty-six, two days after the birth of her sixth child." Child mortality was also very high. Bogislaw Friedrich Dönhoff, the last owner of Quittainen, the estate I ultimately managed, made it into a family shelter and poorhouse after seeing his eleven children die.

My family acquired Dönhoffstadt, the former Wolfsdorf, after a similar tragedy. The previous owner, von Rautter, lost fifteen children in the plague epidemic of 1586; only one daughter survived, and she married a Dönhoff. (Dönhoffstadt was lost to the family when the last Dönhoff of that line was killed in a duel in 1810, at the age of twenty.)

The letters and documents in the attics of old houses like

Steinort, some of them stored there more than a hundred years ago, are revelations. As a rule, the immediate survivors are not much interested: "What if anything worthwhile do you expect to find in letters by Uncle X and Aunt Y?" But generations later, when all that "meaningless stuff" has become history, some great-grandchild will pore over these memorabilia or hire an expert to do so. Of course, such papers are found only in houses that have been in the same family for generations.

The mother of the above-mentioned Uncle Carol, Anna, née Countess Hahn, was interested not only in matters relating to society but also in history. Among the papers in the Steinort attic, she discovered the diaries of one Ernst Ahasverus, a grandson of Ahasverus, written in French. Ernst Ahasverus had seen thirty years' service as chamberlain to Queen Elisabeth Christine, spouse of Frederick the Great, and his critical, amusing comments are a mine of information about life at the Prussian court. (The first of four volumes of these diaries was published in 1906; more recently a single volume, edited by Haug von Kuenheim, appeared.) Other parcels included eight hundred letters from Prince Heinrich, Frederick the Great's brother, to Ernst Ahasverus.

One of Ahasverus Lehndorff's great-granddaughters was married to my great-grandfather August Philipp Dönhoff, and Ahasverus's great-grandson Carl fought in the Napoleonic Wars under General von Yorck. In December 1812, Carl rode sixty miles over icy roads from Gumbinnen to Tauroggen in a single day to bring Yorck word that the Prussian states had agreed—in the Convention of Tauroggen — to retract their involuntary pledge of support to Napoleon. In the course of these events, Carl formed a cavalry regiment that was financed almost entirely by the Prussian ranks and that acquitted itself most honorably in the wars of liberation of 1813–14.

The Convention of Tauroggen proclaimed the neutrality

Amélie Dönhoff, my grandfather's sister, lady-in-waiting at the Imperial court at Potsdam. This picture, taken in 1856, is one of the earliest daguerreotypes.

of the Prussian corps—in other words, it made official Prussia's leaving Napoleon's side, a move initiated by General von Yorck with the Russian General Diebitsch. Although it was welcomed in East Prussia, there were also misgivings, for at first it was not clear whether the Prussian King, Frederick William III, and the Russian Emperor, Tsar Alexander I, would agree to this *renversement des alliances*. The threat of French retaliation and, as a result, possibly even greater devastation than had already been inflicted, could not be ruled out. Would the Russians send in enough troops to prevent such an eventuality? And what was to become of Königsberg?

On December 23, 1812, Amélie Lehndorff, née Dönhoff, wrote from Königsberg to her son Carl at Steinort:

> The town is swarming with unfortunate victims. The streets are teeming with French generals and colonels in all sorts of disguises, some even wearing hats of farm women, and half-dead of hunger and cold. . . . Yesterday I saw Prussian troops enter in orderly fashion. All this makes me fear that they plan to defend the city. Sometimes I think that the Russians do not even intend to pursue the French, because they are moving so slowly.

On December 31, she wrote:

> We thought that they [the retreating French army] were being pursued by Cossacks, and from day to day we prepared ourselves for dreadful scenes in our poor city, for arson and plunder, but instead of Cossacks we found returning French troops, fresh and newly outfitted,

marching in order under my window. It was said that they were advancing toward the Russians, but nothing more has been heard about it, and they seem to have disappeared. As to the Cossacks, on the other hand, they are said to be everywhere except here in Königsberg.

Some days later, on January 4, 1813, August Philipp Dönhoff, Carl Lehndorff's brother-in-law, noted in his diary:

> When I came back to Friedrichstein today I found the house full of Russians, Cossacks, and hussars, among them a certain Prince Tartar, a Count Koschkull, and numerous Cossack officers. Every room was filled, and breakfast was served all day long. They were all very polite and considerate. In the evening General Kutuzov and Colonel Tettenborn and fifteen officers were expected. . . . Somebody who had been to Königsberg reported that the Tauroggen Convention had filled the Russian army with enthusiasm: the Prussian officers and men had torn off their French medals and decorations in front of their [the Russians'] eyes and thrown them away.

Everyone realized, he wrote, that a great deal was at stake. After all, Prussia had pledged Napoleon military allegiance; Napoleon's brother, the King of Naples, was still in Königsberg, as was Marshal McDonald; and the Prussian King had not yet given his agreement.

East Prussia continued to suffer extreme poverty for decades after the end of the Napoleonic Wars. Over a period of thirty years, my great-grandfather, who had borne the

Cossack invasion of Friedrichstein with such equanimity, scrupulously entered each and every expenditure in slim notebooks, in French. For years the entries under "Clothing" mentioned only "resoled shoes" and "turned collars." Under "Entertainments" he recorded drinking wine with his Dohna cousins in Königsberg and an occasional glass of beer.

Even if one looks at the history of the land only from the perspective of a single estate like Friedrichstein, one can see how defenselessly it and its people were battered by wars for centuries. The only period of peace and prosperity it enjoyed were the years after the end of the Franco-Prussian War of 1870–71. Of course those years also spelled the end of the old Prussia. The then owner of Friedrichstein—my grandfather—lamented this change. His sister, who was lady-in-waiting at Potsdam and carried on a thirty-year-long political correspondence with him (four thousand letters were found in the Friedrichstein archive), wrote with indignation and dismay about the greed that overtook Berlin in those heady days.

The recipient of these letters, my grandfather August Heinrich Hermann, had been Prussian delegate to the Frankfurt Assembly in the 1840s, where he waged a long battle against the particularists and for a unified Germany. In March 1848, while chairing the Assembly, he exceeded his mandate and, acting without express authority, pushed through the proclamation for German constitutional rights and a press law abrogating censorship. On March 9, 1848, he made the eagle the official German emblem, and black, red, and gold the colors of the flag. The name of August

Heinrich Dönhoff is also appended to the final far-reaching decisions approved by the Assembly, among them the one of March 31, 1848, proclaiming that it was "the sacred duty of the German people to work with all their might for the reconstitution of the Polish kingdom in order to compensate for the injustice wrought by the partition."

My grandfather Count August Heinrich Hermann Dönhoff, sketched at Sans Souci by his sister Amélie.

THE LEHNDORFFS
OF PREYL

Steinort may have been the Lehndorff family estate, but the family seat of "my" Lehndorffs, Sissi and Heini, the close companions of my youth, was Preyl. Situated on a lake about ten miles north of Königsberg, Preyl had been acquired by Heinrich Lehndorff, founder of this collateral line and brother of Uncle Carol's father. Shortly after 1900 he built the castle, whose unattractive exterior was in keeping with the taste of that era. In 1866 Heinrich Lehndorff had become aide-de-camp and confidant of King (later Emperor) William I, a post he held until the sovereign's death, in 1888.

Lehndorff's oldest son, Manfred, the father of my two companions and the last proprietor of Preyl, was a superb horseman. One of the best dressage riders of his time, he also often raced his horses himself. Life in Preyl centered on horses. Manfred had a racing stable in Königsberg on a tract of land at Carolinenhof, the site of the racetrack. During our school vacations we sometimes accompanied him when he drove off to Königsberg early in the morning with his trap and pair of trotters. The morning workout of the racehorses began at six o'clock, which meant getting up at Preyl by four.

At Carolinenhof we'd be greeted by a confusion of horses, jockeys, and trainers from the various stables waiting for their turn. Either Manfred himself or Ludolf, his head coachman, would draw up the day's workout schedule of the Preyl horses: so-and-so many laps of fast gallop, so-and-so many more at a slower pace—there were endless permutations, depending on which stallion or mare was going to race that Sunday, and in which race.

Heini and Sissi frequently rode in the morning workout; I, not being a good enough rider for that, was relegated to watching. Still I enjoyed it, and even more so the breakfast served at eight o'clock amid an unending stream of shoptalk, for naturally during the workouts everybody kept an eagle eye on the competition.

Two mares, Försterchristel and Balga, were set aside at Preyl for Sissi and me, and since we were allowed to ride by ourselves, we would race each other over the sandy roads. Sissi, a gifted rider taught by her father at an early age, also knew how to train horses.

A favorite winter sport of ours involved harnessing a horse to a string of toboggans, a venture that usually ended in wild confusion. The horse, finding the load it was asked to pull surprisingly light, would take advantage of the situation and bolt. The sleds at the end of the chain were generally the ones to pay the piper; with nobody to steer them, they would be tossed about mercilessly until finally one or another overturned.

I am trying to recall our schooling at Preyl, but all I can

remember are the horses. I no longer even know which of the rooms became our schoolroom. The rooms on the upper floors had numbers, like hotel rooms; I thought this was impersonal and unimaginative. How lovely by comparison the names of the guest rooms at Friedrichstein, which were

Manfred Lehndorff, father of the two dearest friends of my youth and one of the best dressage riders of his day.

engraved on small brass tags attached to the room keys: Family Tree Room, Picture Room, Pfanschmidt Room, Royal Room, the Little and Big General's Room, the last so named in honor of General Louis Dönhoff, my grandfather's brother. In winter these rooms, with their twenty-foot ceil-

My cousin Sissi Lehndorff. In Preyl, horses were at the center of things.

ings, were very cold. As we all know, warm air rises, so the General had a platform built halfway between floor and ceiling, which he could reach by ladder and there settle down snugly in an easy chair.

As to the schooling, I can remember only one of our teachers, a young, unworldly woman by the name of Miss Kobert. Her status as disciplinarian automatically made her a class enemy and in our eyes justified our opposing her; moreover, her inherent timidity opened vast possibilities for mischief. One day in her absence we put one of our brown guinea pigs into her room and peered through the keyhole to watch her reaction. Apparently she had never seen such an animal and mistook it for some sort of rat; panicked, she jumped up on a table, never taking her eyes off the peculiar little creature, while the guinea pig, frightened at finding

Heini Lehndorff, in front of the house at Steinort.

itself in strange surroundings, took cover under the bed and stared at her.

Many years later, long after these childhood days, Heini Lehndorff inherited Steinort, the ancestral estate. This was in 1936, after the death of Uncle Carol, who died childless. Heini moved into that "great wilderness" of the Masurian lakes. With great skill and unflagging energy he modernized the estate, and ran it in model fashion both economically and socially.

I never saw Steinort again after July 20, 1944, a fateful day for Heini and many of my other friends. Both he and I were involved with the group of conspirators against Hitler, I in the organizational aspects of the plot and Heini in its actual execution. I was asked to recruit Heinrich Dohna, whom Stauffenberg and the inner circle of plotters considered was the ideal choice for heading up a future East Prussian government. I was also asked to figure out who would be the potentially useful and potentially dangerous members of the regional Nazi administration then headed by Gauleiter Erich Koch. And finally, if everything went according to plan, I was supposed to try to recruit the commander of the only regional tank regiment not under local military jurisdiction but directly under Berlin's.

East Prussia posed a special problem because of the Führer's headquarters and part of its military leadership being stationed there, in fact in the woods of Steinort. The castle itself had been requisitioned by Foreign Minister Ribbentrop. The assassination plans thus had to be drawn up with great care, and the future chief had to be a forceful personality. Nobody seemed to meet these requirements better than Count Heinrich Dohna of Tolksdorf, a man respected in civilian and military circles alike. He agreed unhesitatingly. Like all the others, he too was executed.

For years I asked myself why he, a man I had recruited, should have died while I was merely interrogated and then released. I learned the reason only later: his name had appeared on the list of people earmarked for positions in a new post-Hitler government, while I, because of my responsibilities at Friedrichstein and Quittainen, had ruled out any active future role for myself.

On July 19, 1944, Heini Lehndorff received word at Steinort, where he was on home leave, that the next day was it. At 7 a.m., shortly before Stauffenberg's bomb exploded, he went to Königsberg to take command of the defense sector there if the assassination attempt was a success. He changed clothes in the woods because he could not risk being seen in uniform by Ribbentrop's security guards.

Upon hearing that the attempt had failed, Heini, depressed and worried, returned to Steinort. He parked his car at a farm some distance from the house, then got on his horse and rode up to Steinort as though returning from a routine inspection of the estate. Next morning when he happened to be standing at an open window and saw the Gestapo drive up, his spontaneous reaction was not to get caught. He vanished as though the earth had swallowed him up. He must have jumped out of the first-floor window to the garden and run down toward the lake. The Gestapo set bloodhounds on his trail, but they lost his scent: being an experienced hunter, he probably ran in the shallow water along the shore.

Later, after having turned himself in to spare his family, he once again escaped from the Gestapo in Berlin, but only for a few days. On September 4th he was hanged on the gallows in the prison yard of Plötzensee. Sissi, who had married my brother Dieter in 1933, lost both brother and husband. She and her young children got out of East Prussia on the last westbound train, and after the war she and the children emigrated to Ireland.

$\mathcal{V}$ACATIONS

Because of the considerable age difference between my four older siblings and me, I spent much more time with my Lehndorff cousins, my contemporaries, than with my own family. Yet strangely enough we did not meet when we were little. My parents occasionally visited Preyl, but it never occurred to them to take me along: in those days one didn't fuss about children. Nor do I remember being taken on trips during the summer vacations, although shortly after the end of the First World War, my mother once did take me along when she went to Switzerland to visit her sister. I remember in particular our stop at Romanshorn, because of the special treat: hot chocolate with cake and whipped cream. This was my first taste of whipped cream: during the First World War my parents had made a point of not living any better than the rest of the people. This first indulgence of mine had dreadful consequences, for no sooner had we set foot in the elegant house of the Thiele-Winklers than I found I could not keep the delicacies down. I wanted the ground to open up under me. After all, hadn't I been told over and over again to be on my best behavior?

My older brothers and sisters and I once went to stay at the Hotel Huis ter Duin at Noordwijk, in Holland. I remember their excitement on the way back, their plans about all the things they would do once they got home. One of my brothers said he'd go snipe-hunting; my oldest sister was going to saddle up her beloved mare. I was still too young for any such plans, and moreover I was so disgusted with that "stupid hotel" we'd stayed at that I was unable to share their elation. On our last day there, being angry about some reprimand or other at dinner, I bit a chunk out of a delicate water goblet. My governess, knowing full well that my aunt had given me five marks for the trip—I think it was the very first money of my own—said that I would have to pay for the glass out of my own pocket. I thought to myself, So what? I'm so rich I can afford to break six glasses.

No doubt to dramatize the situation, the waiter was sent to the mâitre d'hotel to find out what a new glass would cost. The word he brought back was "five marks"; this startling information may account for my early indifference to money and the feeling that it was pointless to chase after such an ephemeral worldy good.

Vacations away from home were as unwelcome as the visits of other children to Friedrichstein. We felt that we could easily dispense with both. What made us doubly eager to get back home were our animals; we couldn't wait to find out how they had fared in our absence. Once, when I was confined to bed for three days, a young fox I had somehow managed to tame had run away. He never returned, and I doubt that he survived; an animal removed from its natural setting has trouble readjusting. A young roebuck I adopted and named Peter suffered a similarly sad fate. Apparently his mother had been killed by a pack of dogs, and our farmhands found the half-starved young buck and brought him to us. I bottle-fed him, and gradually little Peter became so attached to me that he followed my every step. When he grew too big to remain indoors, we put him in a large fenced-in enclosure in the tree-lined family burial ground above the park. There he thrived, but lacking a worthy rival after he grew his first antlers, he attacked the gardener, who then presented my mother with an alternative: either let the burial plot be ruined or get rid of Peter. Faced with this potent threat, Mother decided that Peter would have to be set free, and so, with a heavy heart, I led him to the woods. My brother Christoph came along to help me chase him away, but it was hopeless. With giant leaps Peter kept coming back to us, and finally followed us home. We were told that we would have to turn him over to one of the forest rangers, and that was that.

Foxes and deer were not our only pets. We also had less noble creatures, like rabbits and guinea pigs and dogs. Above all dogs. Christoph had a much-loved dachshund by the name of Hexe, a passionate hunter. With the help of Hexe and two other dachshunds belonging to one of the rangers, we sometimes cornered foxes in their holes. Foxes and badgers occasionally live in the same hole. We wouldn't bother badgers, but foxes were chicken thieves and thus enemies that from time to time had to be got rid of.

If after slithering into a hole the dogs found a fox, they would announce it by making a special noise, and then everything got very exciting. The question was, would the fox "jump"—that is, come out of the hole to be shot by one of the hunters lying in wait nearby? And if so, would the dogs manage to get out safely? There was no guarantee that they would. While making their way in the underground maze, they might come to a dead end or find their escape blocked by the fox. When that happened, they signaled their distress by the way they barked, and we would then try to free them with the help of an axe and a shovel. However, given obstructions like tangled tree roots, we did not always succeed, or if we did manage to cut through the roots we might find that the dogs were no longer where we had heard them.

We always had dogs, and always different ones. My mother had a strange passion for changing breeds: Hungarian sheep dogs, Irish setters, German boxers. The first ones I remember were Newfoundlands, a whole pack housed in a kennel. Once—I was about five at the time—I opened the door of their kennel and all of them bolted out, jumping over me like horses over a fallen rider. Later we had greyhounds. I also have an unpleasant memory connected with them. One morning we all left the house, and the dogs, which were recent acquisitions not yet used to their surroundings, stayed in Mother's bedroom. They of course snooped around everywhere, and in the course of their investigations discovered a big box of chocolate-coated laxative pills. They must have liked them, for they ate every last one; we were greeted by the evidence of their feast when we returned that night.

Next came a series of Great Danes. The first one, Monk, a big, yellow-coated, scary fellow, arrived in a huge crate. After being freed from his prison he was put in a basket in Mother's bedroom. When she went to her bed that night, she found Monk had preceded her and, growling and showing his teeth, he defended his position. Mother was forced to spend the night on the couch.

Dogs were not her only passion. She also acquired exotic breeds of chickens. Oringtons, Plymouth Rocks, and a variety of others inhabited the chicken house supervised by one Mrs. Olschewski. The Plymouth Rocks were splendid, gray-black speckled birds. They hadn't been there long when we hit on the idea of trying to see what would happen if we fed them bread soaked in alcohol. The effect was startling, particularly with the cock, a fine specimen of a fellow, who sopped it up. Before we knew what was happening, he got up on one leg and started crowing nonstop. Lunchtime came and we couldn't stay around to see what happened next; then we forgot all about it. To our consternation, Mrs. Olschewski appeared that evening to tell Mother that she'd had to slaughter the cock because he had suddenly taken sick: "What do you mean sick?" "He was shaking all over and reeling about." We quickly made ourselves scarce.

$\mathcal{T}$HE FAMOUS STUD FARM
AT TRAKEHNEN

From time to time some Lehndorffs from Trakehnen joined our threesome—Sissi, Heini, and me. Equerry Count Siegfried Lehndorff, head of the Trakehnen stud farm, was the father of six sons and one daughter, the oldest of whom was about our age. Their mother, incidentally, was the daughter of the arch-conservative Mr. von Oldenburg-Januschau, a neighbor and political ally of Hindenburg. My father did not hold him in high regard; the man was too reactionary for his taste, but most people found his down-to-earth manner refreshing. "The troughs never change, only the cattle that feed from them," he was wont to say with reference to the Reichstag elections. In an address before the Reichstag he once said, "The King of Prussia and Emperor of Germany must have the power at any moment to order a lieutenant to take ten men and close the Reichstag"—hence the phrase "a lieutenant and ten men" entered into the language of German politics.

Our occasional get-togethers with these other Lehndorffs offered many opportunities for all sorts of activities: hide-and-seek in the dark corners of the house at Preyl was a great favorite. Stealing crows' nests was also very exciting.

This involved climbing up pine trees with the help of irons like those used by telephone linesmen. And horses now began to play a big role in our lives. Occasionally we spent part of our vacation at Trakehnen, the renowned breeding farm founded in 1732 by Frederick William I, father of Frederick the Great. After the King had the stock of various other East Prussian stud farms moved to Trakehnen, its holdings grew to more than a thousand horses, including five hundred mares. Over the years land kept on being added, and by the time we got to know Trakehnen it occupied about fifteen thousand acres and had three hundred and fifty select breeding mares divided into groups by color: chestnuts, duns, blacks, and a mixed group.

I had always loved horses, but at Trakehnen I learned to appreciate the nobility of these highborn creatures. Each of the twenty choice stallions had his own pavilion and run and was treated as an individual. Like the aristocracy in the *Almanac de Gotha*, the ancestry of these horses could be traced for generations. A life-size bronze sculpture of one of these select animals, a stallion by the name of Tempelhüter, stood in front of Uncle Siegfried Lehndorff's office building. When the Russians came they shipped it to Moscow, where it now stands in front of an agricultural institute.

When I was at Trakehnen, I was fascinated by a particular stallion named Master Magpie. He was so high-strung that he had to be muzzled to keep him from taking bites out of himself; his body was covered with hairless scars. I was also much taken by two legendary white stallions, Cancara and Nana Sahib, Cancara's grandfather. One time Cancara, spotting the pack of hounds of a drag hunt, jumped over a

picket fence to join the galloping horses. The six-foot wall of
Nana Sahib's enclosure had to be raised after he jumped
over it.

Trakehnen was an incredibly impressive place—old avenues of trees, white picket fences, green meadows, and
noble horses as far as the eye could see. No one who has ever
been in a hunt there, who witnessed the intensity and spirit
of the horses as they took the obstacles, can ever forget it.

Only one of the six Lehndorff boys survived the war:
Hans, a physician and the author of a very special book,
*Token of a Covenant: Diary of an East Prussian Surgeon,
1945–47*. His brothers were all killed in the war, the youngest at the age of nineteen; the oldest, who was exempted
from military service because three of his brothers had died
in the war, and his mother, who had just been liberated from
a Nazi prison, were shot when the Russians marched into
East Prussia. As I mentioned earlier, Heini Lehndorff, the
cousin from Preyl, was executed at Plötzensee; his only
brother had been killed in Russia shortly before his twenty-
fifth birthday. Hitler's war brought devastation to the families in East Prussia. My oldest sister's two sons, not yet
twenty, and my other sister's only son, who had just turned
twenty, all died in the war.

Yet in those days after the First World War, whether at
Friedrichstein, Preyl, or Trakehnen, we were a happy group
of youngsters, riding or hunting or taking dancing lessons
at Preyl with a teacher brought from town. But we were also
strictly disciplined: punishment followed swiftly on the
heels of misdeeds. I once was made to stay at home while a
tutor took the others to Königsberg to see a film. It would

have been my very first movie and I had looked forward to it with great excitement. However, the evening before this momentous occasion, I had locked my cousin Heini Lehndorff in the ice cellar during a game of hide-and-seek and thoughtlessly bolted the door from the outside, then just as thoughtlessly forgot all about it. A good samaritan, hearing Heini's cries, rescued the half-frozen victim. The account of the rescue was made public by the good samaritan, not by the victim, for that would have violated our code of honor. I naturally accepted the Draconian punishment with a show of indifference, for that, too, was part of our unwritten code: begging for mercy was considered undignified.

The ice cellar in question adjoined the kitchen. Built according to the latest technological standards, it was a large, windowless tiled chamber big enough to hold sides of beef, a variety of game, and shelves of preserved foods. Next to it, behind an iron grate, was a dark keep filled with large blocks of ice.

$\mathscr{C}$USTOMS AND OBLIGATIONS

Moving between Friedrichstein and Preyl meant being subject to different rules of behavior, a fact that early on in our lives gave us insight into the relativity of authority. The taboos at Preyl were very different from those at Friedrichstein. In Preyl, for example, we were not allowed to set foot in the kitchen, and eating between meals was forbidden. Consequently, we stole eggs from the chicken coop and sugar from the pantry, and in an old stove in a deserted room in the garden shed we made meringues. We realized that when faced with arbitrary rules, pragmatism was called for. We concluded that what really mattered was accepting basic principles whose immutable values were beyond question.

As I mentioned earlier, the daily morning services at Friedrichstein were attended by everyone: the housemaids, the Misses Schikor and Quednau, our butler, Fritz, and one of his assistants, as well as by us children. Because we realized that this ceremony was part of our life there, we accepted it without demurring. Going to church on Sunday was also obligatory. All of us, parents included, walked down the long tree-lined road to Löwenhagen, for naturally the coachman was not to be disturbed on Sundays. The parents, getting an early start, would lead the way, followed somewhat later by the younger children, and the big ones on bicycles brought up the rear. Since biking up to the church was forbidden—we were supposed to walk in a dignified manner—they would hide their bikes in the bushes on the outskirts of the village.

The pastor lived in Löwenhagen, and when we went by his house on the way to the railroad station we greeted him respectfully. When we saw him at the window working on his sermon, we would bow or curtsy whether he saw us or not. If we rode by in our elegant coach, he could not but notice us, because on the cobblestones a fast vehicle with good springs sounded very different from the peasant carts. To this day I can still hear the sound of those carts on the cobblestones, just as I can still hear the pebbles hitting the wheel spokes when Grenda, driving up to the front gate, spurred the horses on as, with great gusto, he rounded the curve.

Following the example set by the court, we had many coaches lined up in the carriage house. There were one-horse and two-horse carriages of all sizes and degrees of splendor, also traps and a coupé used only for funerals or in case of illness or if His or Her Excellency, as the people called my parents, had to travel in very bad weather.

Grenda, who had a great sense of the dramatic, never tired of telling the story of how he was dispatched to bring the doctor from Königsberg when I was born: "His Excellency came to me and said, 'It's starting—harness the horses and ride as fast as you can, even if it kills them.'" Accordingly, Grenda raced off, picked up Professor Unterberger at Königsberg and was back at the house, a distance of about twelve miles, in a mere three hours. Like all my brothers and sisters I was born at home in Friedrichstein.

We, of course, had to care for and clean up after our animals—dogs and rabbits—ourselves. The principle of helpfulness was so deeply instilled in us that even now I have the reflexive impulse to jump up if someone drops something or seems in need of assistance.

We had to greet all adults, regardless of social station: the pastor, the choirmaster who taught at the village school and played the organ in church on Sunday (the deference shown him was slightly below that shown the pastor), and the workers, which we would have done anyway, without being told. We knew all of them, and many—the cart drivers, for example—were our bosom friends. At harvest time the drivers let me ride along with them from stack to stack on the four-horse wagons; I would sit proudly on the left rear horse and watch out that the two front horses did not get stuck in the rutted fields and that they moved on to the next stack on command. If my attention flagged, there'd be a lot of swearing and I'd be banished for a few days. We learned many useful things from these stern taskmasters—like the art of spitting, for instance. We all mastered it, and once I even managed a distance of thirteen feet. The only thing I never learned was how to snap the four-horse whip. On the other hand, I was the envy of my siblings because I could whistle through my fingers. They got even by spreading the rumor that I had learned this trick on Grenda's fingers.

THE ORIGIN
OF EAST PRUSSIA'S
LANDED ESTATES

Almost every generation left its imprint on the castle; only one room, on the upper floor above the big garden room, was never finished, not even painted. It remained in its skeletal stage and was dubbed the Jumble Room. There generations of Dönhoffs stored furniture and packing cases filled with objects they were either collecting or for which they had no immediate use. We children enjoyed rummaging there.

Much later, when I was grown-up and working on my doctoral dissertation, the Jumble Room turned out to hold a treasure trove of invaluable documents. My dissertation, which dealt with the origin of these types of large landholdings, was subtitled *"Von der Ordenszeit bis zur Bauernbefreiung"* ("From the Era of the Knightly Orders to the Era of Rural Emancipation"). Among the documents I found were the complete ledgers of Friedrichstein's main administration going back to 1790, as well as some extremely interesting French-language diaries kept by my great-grandfather from 1790 to 1815, covering the "French era" and the wars of liberation, as well as his negotiations with Napoleon about war indemnification payments. Like everything else, these documents were destroyed in 1945.

When and how did these large holdings in East Prussia originate? When the Knights of the Teutonic Order crossed the Vistula River in the thirteenth century to settle in the vast forests to the east, their main concern was the defense of the land. Unable to afford a standing army, the Order made knightly service a precondition for the acquisition of land, thus creating a class that, in exchange for service in time of war, was given land. For each forty hides of land (a hide was equal to seventeen hectares, or forty-two acres), the Order demanded heavy horseman's service; that is to say, an occupant of forty hides (about seventeen hundred acres) was obliged to serve in full armor, equipped with heavy weapons and "a horse outfitted in keeping with his armor, accompanied by two additional horsemen." The obligation of occupants of fewer than forty hides was limited to light weapons and only one horse.

Initially the Teutonic Knights reserved the right of land ownership to themselves, and handed out estates only as liens, but as the Order's economic situation deteriorated and its debts to mercenaries and other creditors mounted, it was forced to cede the land to settle its debts. Thus began a second phase, in which the Order was forced to sell or mortgage its estates, thereby expanding the scope of private ownership.

The first Dönhoff, Magnus Ernst, came from Livonia and settled in East Prussia in 1620. After returning to Germany as Polish ambassador to the courts of Saxony and Brandenburg, he acquired the revenue office Waldau on the Pregel in redemption of a lien. In 1666 his son Friedrich bought the basic stock of the Friedrichstein estates for the sum of 25,000 taler "with all the appurtenances and revenues, all rights and privileges, jurisdictions, great and small, also roads, other domains, hunts and fisheries, inns and licenses, mills and millsteads. . . ."

Magnus Ernst Dönhoff, voivode of Pernau.

Over the years he bought additional estates for cash. Apparently he was able to make these cash purchases because he held official positions; income from land was small and thus land prices were low, whereas government offices were comparatively well paid. According to his records, his income for the five-year period 1691–95 as prefect and governor of the Fortress Memel was about the same as from the 10,500-acre Friedrichstein estates: 27,000 taler each.

As a matter of fact, liens were generally disadvantageous for the creditor because a debtor who repaid his debt had to be compensated for all expenses incurred during the period of the loan; most often the creditor was unable to do so. Fixed interest rates were as yet unknown. It was assumed that the yield from the mortgaged property would be equivalent to the yield of the loan, a concept arising out of the barter-economy thinking of that era.

(The transfer of liens, the typical form of credit funding in the Middle Ages, continued well into modern times. Thus, when the city of Bern in the early eighteenth century extended a loan to Austria, the two parties negotiated about the mortgaging of the Austrian "headland" as well as all "sovereign rights," and the prompt transfer of the lien to the creditor. And in 1768 the Republic of Genoa was forced to give the island of Corsica to the French state as a lien.)

Fifty years later, in 1747, Friedrich Dönhoff's grandson acquired the adjacent estates of Borchersdorf and Weissenstein, initially as liens; thirty years later, they became the property of the owner of Friedrichstein. A contemporary chronicle states: "Since both estates are located along the highway, they suffered severe damage because of the war, and large portions were devastated." And with regard to Weissenstein, it goes on to say: "Of thirteen peasants only four are still on their farms, and of these, only two farms are in fairly good condition." The third peasant fled during the war but returned; the estimated value of his scorched home was eighty marks. The fourth, who lost everything, "ran away during the events of the war and stayed in the old city of Königsberg, but was taken back from there and settled on the property." The remaining nine farms were destroyed. Of four it says that nothing was left of the buildings except "some old beams and sticks of firewood." Their worth was an estimated twenty marks. "Of the remaining five land-holdings no buildings stand."

Of all the estates that were purchased in the course of a hundred years and that together formed the Friedrichstein estate, only one, Barthen, was "in superb condition." The reasons for the sale of the others were indebtedness and the poor economic situation, mostly owing to a series of devastating wars with Russia, Poland, and Sweden. Only someone like Otto-Magnus Dönhoff, who built the castle in the early eighteenth century and who held high official posts, could afford to acquire and restore these neglected properties.

Otto-Magnus was first attaché at the German Imperial court, Secretary of State and War, Prussian ambassador at the Peace Congress of Utrecht, lieutenant general and governor of Memel. When he acquired the 5,000-acre estate of Hohenhagen in 1713, its buildings were in a condition of disrepair, most of the people had moved away, and there was hardly any livestock: "The woods were deforested and ruined, the fields uncultivated and unfertilized."

Of all the improvements introduced by him, probably the most noteworthy was the well in the stable. This made it possible for water to be pumped into the drinking troughs, and now in winter the cattle no longer had to be driven to the iced-over pond.

Today we can hardly visualize the primitive state of farming in those days. An excerpt from an eighteenth-century chronicle describes a new chaffing machine at Hohenhagen as a masterpiece of modern technology:

An old draw well in Hohenhagen.

This is the first such machine in all of Prussia. Because no artisan in the land is able to build such a chaffing mill, Count Friedrich Dönhoff brought a millwright by the name of Rammin from Berlin; and in 1750 he, together with Krebs, the miller at Friedrichstein, whom he supervised, made the requisite wooden parts at Friedrichstein. The necessary ironwork was ordered from the most skilled smith at Königsberg, and then it and the woodwork were brought to Hohenhagen and there were affixed to the mill.

This is followed by a complicated description of the mill's simple mechanism:

The mill is pulled by two horses on the ground floor; on the upper floor stands the load from which the knife with one stroke can cut through a twelve-inch densely packed layer of straw. Two persons are needed, one to lead the horses below in a circle, the other on the upper floor to keep replenishing the supply of straw. The strokes of the knife follow in rapid succession and the cut chaff falls into a separate storage chamber through a hole made especially for this purpose.

The chronicler's obvious delight in this machine is understandable, considering that before its introduction many men at each farm worked from dawn to dusk to cut the straw; when the entire supply of straw could be cut at Hohenhagen these men were available for other chores. The cost of this marvel was 200 taler.

For a long time, life in the country continued to be harsh

and frugal. Eighty years after the invention of that chaffing machine, in 1830, the budget of Friedrich Dönhoff's grandson showed an income of 34,997 taler and expenditures of 33,946. The largest sum listed under expenses, 17,733 taler, is for "repaid capital"; the next, 5,408 taler, is for the education and support of seven children, followed by "interest payments to my family, 4,018 taler, and interest for capital loans, 4,998 taler." Other listed items involve minimal sums— "personal expenditures" (clothes, books, travel, presents, tips, wine, postage, and similar items), 373 taler; "upkeep of the household" (spices, rice, sugar, salt, herring, soap, lighting, work clothes for the staff), 224 taler.

For the owner of a 15,000-acre estate this does not seem opulent. True, the economy was still reeling from the aftershocks of the Napoleonic Wars. The sum of 150 million taler, a then unimaginably large amount of money, had to be paid to France for war indemnification.

ＤISEASE AND WAR DEVASTATE
THE ESTATES

Fate has never been kind to East Prussia. Between 1708 and 1711 plague wiped out more than forty percent of its population; an estimated 250,000 people out of a total of 600,000 died in that period, which explains the many abandoned farms and the shortage of farm labor. Then, between 1756 and 1763, during the Seven Years' War, troop billeting and the requisitioning of supplies and livestock depleted stores and stockpiles. A contemporary document contains this account:

In 1757, after the lost battle of Grossjägersdorf (near Wehlau), the Prussian army retreated westward and for eight days set up camp on the Friedrichstein estates, and the damage they inflicted has been estimated at four thousand taler. Soon thereafter a brigade of the Imperial Russian army set up its headquarters at Friedrichstein and the neighboring villages. In the spring of 1759 the Russian army reappeared, and for many weeks two regiments were spread throughout the estate. When the army finally left the estate, the farmers were forced to furnish fodder and supplies and escort the army for many more weeks. As late as August, 1761, fifteen two-horse carriages with supplies and transports were sent via Kulm to Posen and Silesia, and some of these were under way for more than four months.

In a report by Count Dönhoff to the King dated September 20, 1757, he describes the "considerable damage" his estates suffered at the hands of the looting, marauding soldiery, particularly the Black Hussars. In some of the villages, he wrote, "all the doors were broken, the people beaten, robbed, the buildings in part wantonly destroyed and the supplies, including seed corn, requisitioned."

The estates in East Prussia were a mixture of owner-managed units, often called "the farm," and tenant farms on estate-owned land. In other words, the estate comprised a farm that employed its own workers, and the so-called village, which comprised the tenants, artisans, and laborers, usually with an inn as the social center. The tenants had to work on the estate for one or two weeks doing sharecropping. Most of their leaseholds consisted of two to three hides; in the eighteenth century the rent amounted to between ten and twenty taler per hide. By modern standards the specialized skills listed in the wage ledgers are staggering: mason, carpenter, sawyer, wheelwright, cartwright, cooper, joiner, glazier, pump digger, bricklayer, potter, blacksmith, farrier, ironsmith, coppersmith, plumber, furrier, saddlemaker, harnessmaker, tanner, ropemaker, brushmaker, weaver, cobbler, thatcher, chimney sweep.

It is astonishing that a theory expounded by Georg Friedrich Knapp in his book of 1887—*Die Bauernbefreiung und der Ursprung der Landarbeiter in den älteren Teilen Preussens (Rural Emancipation and the Origin of Farm Labor in the Older Parts of Prussia)*—namely, that "expropriation of the peasants" created East Prussia's great estates, should have survived these hundred years. I suppose it has something to do with widely held preconceptions. In fact, the emancipation edict of October 1807, which made the peasants the proprietors of the land but deprived them of the support of the estates, reduced them to agricultural laborers; the estate owners became more interested in enlarging their pool of rent-paying peasants than in the acquisition of land as such.

The emancipation edict stated: "As of St. Martin's Day, 1810, all serfdom in all our states ceases. After St. Martin's Day, 1810, there exist only free people."

That may have sounded good, but even at the time the implementation of the edict faced a built-in problem: the processing of claims and compensation, which dragged on for years. Peasants went into debt, and when they found themselves in economic trouble, the estate owners did not help them out as they had in the past; many a bankrupt peasant was happy for the estate owner to buy back his land.

Prior to the edict, the estate owners had no choice but to come to the rescue of the peasants if necessary, at times on a massive scale. In the report in which Dönhoff talks of "considerable damage" to the Friedrichstein estates, he also says that the damage suffered by his Eyserwagen estates in the Wehlau district was so great that he was compelled to buy seed and grain for cash for his serfs from the silos of Königsberg and Wehlau to help them survive until the next harvest.

According to official investigation, the loss thus suffered amounted to more than 22,000 taler. In order, however, to provide the Eyserwagen villages with new inventory, considering that of its thirty householders only a few were left with a horse, and many with nothing at all, I had various Jews and entrepreneurs from Poland purchase as much equipment and workhorses for cash as needed to give every householder with four lots a helping hand and at the same time get the farm going again and also to repair or rebuild all the ruined buildings from the ground up.

It is misleading to call this "expropriation."

The freeing of the peasants was not so liberating as the edict of the reformers led one to believe for still another reason: the estate owners retained many of their prerogatives — either because of tradition, because of newly drafted rigorous local regulations, or because of the agricultural labor law introduced in the mid-nineteenth century, which remained in force until the end of the First World War.

An old peasant dwelling in the Pregel Valley.

Moreover, the estate districts were preserved as administrative units, which guaranteed the perpetuation of certain feudal practices, for the owners continued to personify the self-administration in their district. It was they who exercised police powers, for example.

Knapp's assumption that East Prussia's large estates came into being as a result of expropriation may have been due to unfamiliarity with the customary practices of that region; his experience was with the tenant-farming system of western Germany. Contrary to Knapp's theory, in the seventeenth century the owner of Friedrichstein founded nine new villages in the Pregel Valley, in which seventy-seven peasants holding a total of about 2,500 acres were installed as "free farmers," with no obligation to sharecrop. The first four years of their tenancy, in which they had to cultivate the partly marshy land, were rent-free; for the next seven years their rent was twenty groschen per ten acres, and thereafter, one gulden.

ℋOW THE GERMAN DÖNHOFFS BECAME POLISH DÖNHOFFS

Among my discoveries in researching my doctoral dissertation was a suitcase filled with jottings and notes about the

Polish branch of the Dönhoffs, which had died out in the late eighteenth century. (The last two female Dönhoff descendants in Poland died in 1791.) My grandfather, apparently planning one day to make use of this important unevaluated material, had engaged an expert to sort it out. But in 1945 these notes burned, together with all the other documents.

When I was still very young, long before I began work on my dissertation, I became curious about the gold-framed miniatures, on a background of brown velvet, that stood on a table in the garden room at Friedrichstein. All those strange names! There were portraits of Louis XV of France and his wife, Maria Leszczynska, daughter of the Polish King Stanislas Leszczynski; of Stanislas Leszczynski's grandparents; of Gerhard Dönhoff, born 1590, Master of the Prince's household in Poland, and his wife, Princess Sibylle von Brieg und Liegnitz. I did not find out when and how the German Dönhoffs became Polish Dönhoffs until I went through that suitcase and some other boxes in the Jumble Room.

My family migrated from western Germany into the northeastern region between the Vistula River and Lake Peipus in 1330. For centuries, Germans, Poles, Russians, Swedes, and Danes lived and fought there, concluded treaties and made war on each other, and alternately exercised sovereignty, depending on who was subjugating whom at any given time. The Dönhoff family clung to their new home, regardless of who its rulers were: the Teutonic Order, the Church, the Poles, Swedes, Russians, or Prussians.

*Stanislas Ernst Dönhoff (1673–1728),
military commander of Lithuania
and voivode of Plock.*

The Dönhoffs who in the Middle Ages left their old Westphalian home, Dunehof on the Ruhr, and moved east, initially went beyond their later home in East Prussia and settled in Livonia (now part of Latvia); from there they came west to East Prussia in 1620. The first to move east in 1330, with the Order of the Sword, was Knight Hermanus Dönhoff, who was married to a Pappenheim. As the progenitor of a new branch of the family, he built a second Dunehof in Livonia, on the Musa River, south of Riga, and the estate was handed down to the oldest son; the younger male children entered the Order. This branch lived in the area between the Vistula and Lake Peipus for eighteen generations: in Livonia until the death of the last Polish Dönhoff in 1791, and in East Prussia until the entry of the Russians in January 1945.

The Order of the Sword, to which Knight Hermanus apparently felt a greater kinship than to the Teutonic Order (which would have settled him in Prussia), ruled in Livonia for three hundred and fifty years; in 1567 the Poles forced the last head of the Order, Gotthard von Kettler, to sign a writ of submission, and the Order was dissolved. By agreement, the land north of the Düna had to be ceded to Poland, while the land to the south became a secular duchy. Since the Dönhoffs stayed where they were, two branches of the Dönhoff family, German and Polish, thus came into being.

Gert the Old, a seventh-generation Dönhoff, was the first to enter the political arena. He became Lord of the Banner of Livonia, an important office in the fifteenth century, for originally only the sovereign was entitled to carry the banner, the symbol of authority. In times of conflict the Lord of the Banner fought alongside the head of the Order, and in times of peace he helped build its internal administration. Having aligned himself with the Reformation, he became one of the biggest landowners in the country. He died in 1574 in Riddelsdorf.

His portrait at Friedrichstein made a lasting impression on me. It shows him life-size, with a scraggly goatee and a black patch over his left eye. We children were fascinated by him, for we had been told that he lived to be over a hundred and that he lost his eye at the age of seventy when he jumped

Alexander Dönhoff.

over a table to demonstrate his agility to his obese son. The son's portrait hung next to his.

Many foreign titles were appended to the names of the Dönhoffs on the baroque gold-framed miniatures: voivode, starost, castellan, and an occasional general fighting in the Polish army against the Turks. One of these Dönhoffs, Johann Kasimir, was the godson of King Johann Kasimir, the last of the Vasa dynasty to occupy the Polish throne. Johann Kasimir Dönhoff joined the clergy, studied at Rome,

Stanislas Dönhoff, the last proprietor of Dönhoff-stadt, killed in a duel at the age of twenty.

entered the papal court of Innocent XI, was appointed papal nuncio by the Polish King, and ultimately was made a cardinal by the Pope.

Another Dönhoff, Caspar, born in 1587, won the gratitude of King Ladislas IV of Poland because of the satisfactory execution of a mission on the King's behalf. The King had sent him to Vienna to arrange the marriage between himself and Archduchess Cecilia Renata, sister of Emperor Ferdinand III. Caspar was made prince and grand marshal. His three sons married into the great families of Poland: the Radziwills, the Leszczynskis, and the Osalinskis.

Caspar's younger brother Gerhard also proved to be a successful proxy suitor. After the death of Cecilia Renata, Ladislas IV sent Gerhard to Paris to draw up a nuptial agreement with Louise Marie of Nevers Gonzaga, the wealthy daughter of the Duke of Mantua. In gratitude for the success of this second nuptial mission, Gerhard was made castellan of Danzig and Naval and War Commissioner of the Fleet. This made him the only Polish admiral prior to 1918—a purely theoretical office, since no fleet was ever built.

One day quite by accident I discovered that, contrary to our previous assumption, the history of the Polish Dönhoffs had apparently not come to an end in 1791. I was in Poland in my postwar role of journalist, and I took a walk through the cemetery at Povaski, where I came across a gravestone with the inscription "Miecio Denhoff, nine months old, died 1903."

Died 1903? How was this? Coincidentally, a Polish acquaintance of mine, Andrzej Niewiadomski, had also come across this name; his genealogical and historical interest aroused, he decided on his own to look into the matter. Two years later he told me the amusing story he had learned.

It seems that in 1782 Louise-Sophie von Kleist, the fifteen-year-old daughter of the royal Polish chamberlain Ernst-Nicolas von Kleist, was married to a rich, older nobleman, the forty-three-year-old voivode Count Jan-Thaddeus von Syberg. It was a time of national ferment, before the promulgation of the new Polish constitution of 1791, and the house of this young woman became the gathering place of a group of Polish notables. One day the twenty-four-year-old scion of another eminent family, Stanislas Ledóchowski, a comrade-in-arms of the legendary freedom fighter General Thaddeus Kosciusko, came to Louise-Sophie's salon. The two young people fell in love, scandalizing society. Their unorthodox union produced three children, two sons and a daughter, and the parents solved the embarrassing problem of what to name their offspring by calling them Denhoff. After all, the Dönhoffs had died out—so why not? There was no one to object to this irregular but eminently practical solution. The two sons became officers. That is the last thing known about them. The Miecio Denhoff who died in 1903 at the age of nine months, whose grave I saw, must have been a descendant of one of these sons.

$\mathscr{F}$RIEDRICHSTEIN BECOMES AN ENTAILED ESTATE

After 1791, East Prussia was the only region with true Dönhoffs. They had been at Friedrichstein since 1660 and would remain there until 1945. For eight generations the estate was handed down from father to eldest son. Even though by tradition the younger siblings did not exercise any hereditary claims, there was no guarantee that it would remain forever thus. Therefore my grandfather decided, once all debts had been paid (the result of his father's and his almost ascetic frugality), to entail the estate and make its owner a trustee without the right of free disposal. The succession would be restricted to the oldest son; the other children would go empty-handed. The daughters would be given a dowry when they married, and the younger sons suitable educations. Beyond that they would be on their own. However, the children could always find a home there in their old age. The Weimar Constitution of 1919 abolished these entailments. (At the time, there were about thirteen hundred entailed estates throughout Germany.)

In the preamble to the deed of 1859 my grandfather wrote:

I, the current owner of the Friedrichstein estates, August Heinrich Hermann Count Dönhoff, born at Potsdam on October 10, 1797, Royal Prussian Privy Councilor and member of the House of Lords, by converting these estates into entailments, intend with God's help to avert the danger (breakup through division of the inheritance) as far as it is in my power to do so. For many years I have felt compelled to persevere in the pursuit of this objective. After much effort I managed to wipe out the debts incurred by the estates, and I believe that I have succeeded in handing down to my successors a worry-free existence, and to the entire family a base and guiding principle for all time to come.

I hope that the future proprietors will look on this endowment as an abiding challenge and a debt of honor, will feel that their life must be dedicated to more than indolence and pleasure, and that they—just as the endowment itself was made possible only by the sustained practice of strict economy—for their part in like manner will pay serious heed to the preservation, improvement, and expansion of the estate, to the suitable support of its widows and descendants, and to the accumulation of reserves to help out in times of war and other calamities. I call upon the future trustees to remember that they, being relieved of the worry of supporting themselves, have the duty, if they are suited for it, to represent higher interests, particularly the public concerns of the country.

It would not have occurred to any of us to criticize or even in our minds fault the arrangement that discriminated against the younger descendants. We were proud to call this lovely property our home, and we knew that it could never have been preserved had the heirs been free to divide it. My oldest brother, the owner of Friedrichstein, lived extremely modestly himself, but poured huge sums into the renovation of the house. He spent years having the ugly dark-brown stain favored in the nineteenth century removed from the wainscoting, restored its original colors, and replaced the gold paint with gold leaf.

Every summer Alfred Sommerfeld, the restorer of the former royal palaces of Berlin, together with his family, spent four weeks at Friedrichstein supervising its beautification. The restoration was completed shortly before the

A late eighteenth-century etching of Friedrichstein seen from the lake.

outbreak of the Second World War, only to have all this new splendor go up in flames in the spring of 1945 when the Russians marched in.

The social arrangement by which those who enjoyed privileges were in return expected to exhibit greater concern for society than for their own person was reinforced by awareness of being part of a close-knit community. This sort of paternalism might possibly have led egotistical, unstable individuals to abuse their position and their privileges. But then, no society has yet come up with foolproof safeguards against abuse. Human beings are bound to act all too humanly.

Every revolution begins with the promise to do away with the social inequalities of the existing order, to replace oppression with freedom, but it generally does not take long for new forms of injustice to take the place of the old. Once the new laws, regulations, prohibitions, and practices have been put into place, people begin to look for—and find—new loopholes. Moreover, every system seems to come equipped with its own set of temptations. Eschenburg, in his book *Spielregeln der Politik (Rules of the Game of Politics)*, asks:

Why was there hardly any Parliamentary corruption in the Imperial Reich from 1871 to 1918, and so much less in the Weimar Republic, 1918–1933, than today? Was it a higher morality? For one thing, before 1908 the delegates were not compensated; even after 1918 their stipends were very modest, and pensions for delegates were unheard of. Today's professional politicians, on the other hand, demand and receive far more money than their pre-1933 counterparts. Although this system of salaries and pensions is absolutely justified, unstable persons might be swayed by a desire to insure themselves against the possible loss of their position and compensation. This sort of security cannot be guaranteed without some corruption.

Thus, according to Eschenburg, the desire of the people's representatives for the greatest possible measure of independence led dialectically to a new type of dependence.

When I think about it today, my relationship to Friedrichstein seems to have been composed of a hard-to-define mixture of boundless love and a strangely abstract pleasure in ownership, somewhat the way people today love the

Spring thaw in the Pregel Valley.

endangered environment. There is the desire to protect it, to care for it, even to feel responsible for it, not as a private owner but on a higher plane.

Back then, as a child, I would not have been able to define my feelings even this inarticulately, for we do not think about what seems self-evident. Just as animals — the fox and the lynx and birds of prey — stake out their territory and rule over their domain, we children built our retreats in the fields of Friedrichstein. Every fall new huge tree houses went up and rabbit hutches were enlarged or moved to other sites. My older brothers and sisters even built a little house at the edge of the forest, with real windows and a real door, and with a roof no carpenter could have done better. Even though they offhandedly called their house a shack, they set great store by its appearance. They planted a garden in front and built a small bridge across a ditch, with a railing of slender white birchwood cunningly shaped to spell out the initials of the builders.

LAVISH HOSPITALITY, PERSONAL AUSTERITY

Many of the elusive yet typical qualities of East Prussia were, I believe, the product of its unique history. That history gave rise to traditions and customs different from those found in the rest of Germany. Strangely enough, differences in the way of life were found even in parallel social classes — strange because basically there exist internationals not only of workers, but also of intellectuals and of the aristocracy. Similarities within these groups tend to transcend national divisions, and generally their members can readily identify their counterparts in other countries.

I mentioned earlier that in East Prussia the owners of large estates took an active part in administering their properties, while in the West the owners were merely landlords who leased their land to small farmers; it is therefore not surprising to find that the relationship between owner and tenant in these different types of landholding differed as well. In East Prussia it may perhaps have been more paternalistic — or more servile — but at the same time it was closer and more personal, and there was greater interdependence; the parallel age groups of the upper and lower levels knew each other fairly well; this made for a peculiar amalgam of formality and familiarity.

What also seems strange to me when I think about it now is what we today call life-style. Ours back then was characterized by a mixture of lavish hospitality and personal austerity, perhaps best exemplified by the contrast between the opulence of the castle's official rooms and the Spartan simplicity of the family quarters.

In my day the room at the end of the suite along the south pediment facing the park underwent the greatest change. At one time this had probably been my parents' bedroom, but once my oldest brother's passion for restoration won out over the worrying matter of costs, he called in Berlin's foremost restorer of Prussian mansions. Work was begun, and after the paint was stripped from the wall panels, well-preserved frescoes were found depicting a group of obviously contented men sitting around a table on strangely shaped green chairs. When Fritz, our invaluable butler, saw this, he exclaimed, "But those are the chairs stored in a closet in the attic!" They were brought down and, lo and behold, they were indeed the very chairs.

Soon we were given another unexpected nugget of information. Upon seeing the chairs when he was visiting us, Professor Arnold Hildebrandt, curator of the Hohenzollern

The garden room and the rooms adjoining to the north, leading to my father's study.

Museum of Berlin, said, "These are copies of the chairs of Frederick William I's Tobacco Council," and added, "This was probably a meeting in honor of the King, perhaps on the occasion of a visit by him." We decided to turn this room with the strange frescoes into our "small" dining room, and that's what it remained until the end.

The adjoining rooms were all of great splendor: first was the small room with the *art nouveau* tapestry embroidered by my mother in 1900; after that came the Red Room. It had a connecting door to the back stairs and was used by the staff when they came to see us to discuss a problem or offer a suggestion. Then came the Green Parlor, its walls deco-

The garden room—the center of the house—and the rooms adjoining to the south.

rated with those tapestries specially woven for it in Flanders; after that came the garden room with its beautiful plasterwork ceiling and walls.

In my childhood the dark walls of the dining room were covered with rows of eighteenth- and nineteenth-century Dutch paintings in black frames, with not an inch of space between them. Since the pictures themselves were rather dark, this gloomy chamber contrasted sharply with the sun-filled garden room adjacent. But once the layers of brown paint were stripped off the dining-room panels, we found that they had originally been painted a wonderful Chinese dragon red. The wife of Professor Hildebrandt, née Cranach, a painter who lived up to her illustrious maiden name, painted Chinese symbols on some yellow silk we had bought, and helped turn this forbidding room into a most original, cheerful place.

Adjacent to the dining room was a suite of three more rooms, the walls of one also covered with Flemish tapestries. The last of these was my father's study. I can still see him sitting there. Originally called the "judging chamber," a designation going back to the days when my forebears exercised patrimonial jurisdiction, this room had a separate door leading to the outside. Through it came people wishing to consult the judge summoned for this purpose from Königsberg to adjudicate disputes among the peasants— matters of inheritance, property, and the like. Later, in my brother's day, this part of the castle was turned into an apartment for the chief forest ranger.

We children were housed in very simple little rooms. Apparently some time back a section of the upper story had been divided in half horizontally. Since the rooms were originally twenty feet high, this posed no problem, but as a result of the alteration the windows of the boys' rooms, which were on the top, were level with the floor. We girls also had our own rooms, and felt privileged because ours, being on the lower level, had more light.

The furniture in these rooms was also uniformly Spartan: a bed, a wardrobe, a washstand and basin, a pitcher and pail. No running water. My older sisters had an object I admired and coveted: a white china rabbit with red eyes, long ears, and a built-in clock. I thought this piece of trash was an extraordinary and most valuable work of art.

Sanitation left much to be desired. Every floor had a closet housing the essential facility. Bathrooms were later additions. In my childhood only my parents had a bathroom. The guest rooms, which were very large and opulent, had a different arrangement: every evening, a wide-rimmed circular tub with a spigot for pouring off the bathwater would be set up in each, next to which were put two large cans, somewhat like watering cans, filled with warm water, and a chair draped with a bath towel the size of a sheet.

I have no idea whether this contrast between luxury and personal austerity was planned or whether, as I suspect, it just came about. I think it expressed the temperament of the owners—and maybe a bit of bad conscience as well. Perhaps they wished to compensate for their privileged position and the splendor of their regal house by stressing the simplicity of their own life. This, incidentally, was also reflected by the food served the family: we ate well only when we had guests. Father had wine; we children drank water brought daily to the kitchen in a large, horse-drawn aluminum tank. In winter the water came from a pump in the yard; in summer, as a concession to hygiene, from a pump in the old village where the water was said to be cleaner. It was indeed clearer, but on hot days its odor was so offensive that we had to hold our breath when we drank. We'd have liked to have held our noses too, but didn't: we'd only have been told not to be so fussy.

When I am asked where I am from, I instinctively answer East Prussia—not Hamburg, where I have lived, and hap-

pily so, for more than forty years. The reason: I miss the countryside, the landscape, the animals of my lost world. And also the sounds, those myriad sounds, that are indelibly etched in my memory—all the sounds we heard at dusk as we sat on the terraced steps in front of the house and watched the swallows dart around and the bats perform their zigzag dance. And a little later, as darkness fell, we could hear the screech owls hoot. Later still in the evening, we'd walk to the pond where countless frogs staged a fantastic concert, so noisy that we had to raise our voices to make ourselves heard.

There is a spit of land in Hamburg near Blankenese that is almost like East Prussia, and although I enjoy living there, I have yet to hear a frog in the meadow. Sometimes it is summer before I see the first butterfly, and at night the only thing I hear is the whoosh of a car driving by or the slamming of a car door. It is a poor little world.

Most of us undoubtedly tend to idealize our childhood, and we would probably have trouble saying exactly what it was that made it unique. In my case my relationship with my brothers and sisters played a significant role. Ours was a rare kind of closeness. We used to say jokingly—but in a way we also meant it—that when we get old we'd get rid of the outsiders we had married and move back together again.

When one of my older brothers returned from a trip, we would all come back to Friedrichstein and he would give a report of everything he had done and seen, beginning with his departure from the station. The stories we liked best of all were those of my oldest brother, who spent the golden 1920s in Berlin. When he told of the wonderful productions of Max Reinhardt, of the dramatic or poetic subtleties of a particular play, we listened with bated breath and felt as though we were seeing it ourselves. It was almost better than being there in person.

THE END OF
OUR CAREFREE LIFE

There came a day when our threesome, Sissi and Heini Lehndorff and I, suddenly and inexplicably split up. Heini was sent off to Rossleben to a boarding school, Sissi to a school in Montreux, and I was supposed to be tutored at home with my cousin Huberta Kanitz. This plan, however, was never realized.

One day that autumn, shortly after my cousin came to Friedrichstein, we all went on a trip to the Baltic. We were riding in two cars; the adults were in a car driven by my oldest brother, and since the driver of the other car, the one we children were in, was unfamiliar with the area, he followed my brother's lead. We'd had a wonderful day, and by the time we started back home it was beginning to get dark. We got to Königsberg in a thunderstorm, with very poor visibility. We children — my cousin, young Franz Coudenhove from Austria, two young Swiss, a brother and sister by the name of Lindenmann, and I — were singing and chatting when suddenly we heard our driver cry out. In the next moment, the car overturned, slid down a ravine, and water started pouring in. It occurred to me that we had probably fallen into the Pregel River.

The car was not watertight—it was a convertible with a canvas roof—and the driver, so he told us later, was caught in a whirlpool. It was sheer chaos. We felt a thud as the car came to rest on the river bottom thirty feet down. In no time at all I realized my breath was gone and I was swallowing water.

It's incredible how one's thoughts flash through the mind in the face of imminent death. How can people say, I wondered, that drowning is a quick death when my God, it was taking forever. And then I thought how sad it would be for the people back home to see five children laid out next to one another in the main hall. Then, at what seemed like the very end, my hand suddenly discovered a small space between the canvas roof and the body of the car. I groped around, slid through the opening, and pushed blindly to the surface for what seemed like an eternity.

Finally above water, I could see the headlights of a car shining down toward us and heard my brother call out my name. Had it not been for that, I would surely have drowned, for I was completely exhausted and confused. But when I heard him call me I gathered all my strength and dog-paddled toward the embankment where the rescuers had draped their coats. With my last ounce of strength, I clutched at one of these lifelines and was pulled up. My brother later told me I was the last to come out alive; I'd been under water for about five minutes. The bodies of the two smallest children, Huberta Kanitz and the twelve-year-old Franz Coudenhove, were recovered later. The driver and the two Lindemanns were already out by the time I surfaced.

The poor passengers of the lead car must have been every bit as frightened as we. This is my brother's report about the tragic incident:

At the junction with the Pregel where the road veers sharply to the right, I suddenly realized that I could no longer see the car with the children which had been right behind me. Something dreadful obviously must have happened. I quickly turned back and drove up to the quay, which, I now saw for the first time, was not marked off by either a chain or a raised walk. On the opposite bank of the river stands a lamp, and the unfamiliar driver must have headed toward it. When we trained our headlights on the surface of the river I saw concentric circles forming. Then a hat appeared, and a little later a person, then two more and again two more. And after that nothing for a long time.

The next day coffins stood in the garden room — the very center of the house not only structurally but historically and emotionally as well — not the six I had imagined, yet two nonetheless. In this room everyone dear to us had lain in state — my sister Christa, my mother, my father, his father, his father's father, going back for generations — all except the last proprietor of Friedrichstein, who lies buried in foreign soil in the East. All the family weddings and baptisms and my confirmation had been celebrated in this room.

The accident at Köngisberg naturally shattered my hitherto fairly untroubled existence. The family, fearing it might scar me for life, sought to make up for my loss. However, adults being adults, they only succeeded in dealing me yet another blow by sending me to boarding school in Berlin, one of those girls' institutions specializing in rules and restrictions. The school did not even have its own teaching staff. Classes were held at a nearby school; to get there we had to march through the streets in double file, silently praying that no one we knew would see our ridiculous procession. The one positive thing to come out of my two years' stay in that school was a lasting passion for intellectual pursuits. The seed was planted not by the school itself but by a visitor, Ursula von Kranold, the niece of the headmistress. (I never saw her again and I don't even know whether I have spelled her name correctly.) She delivered a lecture on the philosopher Hermann Keyserling that changed my life. I asked her to let me read the manuscript of her talk, and I came away filled with awed fascination that an "ordinary person" could discover and formulate ideas like his. I decided then and there that that was what I would like to do one day. I had read a lot, but only works of literature; this was my first exposure to philosophy.

Apart from this important revelation, my life in that school was the very antithesis of my former freedom. I took advantage of every opportunity to rebel and thus became something of a ringleader. To my dismay, I was made head of the student body even though I was one of the youngest girls, and this meant taking on responsibilities in an institution that filled me with profound misgivings. I later learned that mine was the school's last graduating class before the headmistress, Mrs. Lindeiner, closed the school. I like to think that our rebelliousness played a part in her decision.

The school where we attended classes was another matter. For me it became a sort of super penal institution, for up to that time I hadn't had any kind of systematic instruction. None of my previous tutors or so-called teachers—there must have been more than a dozen—had given me a solid education. My entrance exam was a catastrophe: in my German history essay I confused the Great Elector with Frederick the Great; in my French *dictée* I made thirty-three mistakes; and of five math problems I didn't understand four and was unable to solve the one I did tackle. I no longer remember the other subjects, but I am sure I did no better in any of them. The teachers were dumbfounded by the depth of my ignorance. Generously ascribing my lack of the most elementary knowledge to the fact that "the child has suffered a terrible shock," they admitted me to my proper grade where, with the help of private tutors and by a great deal of effort, I managed to keep up with the class.

The next three years, until my graduation, I attended school at Potsdam. There I was free, lived at the house of friends, and went to a school where I was the only girl in my class. So at an early age this sequence of tragedy and mishap taught me the chanciness of fate; it was a fitting early instruction in what life held in store for me.

$\mathcal{J}$OURNAL
OF A RIDE
THROUGH
MASURIA *

*This and the following section are taken from my
book *Namen die keiner mehr nennt* (*Names No Longer
Spoken Of*). I have added them here because through
them one can learn a little more about East Prussia
and about what became of Friedrichstein. This Jour-
nal was written in 1941 for my brother Pieter, Sissi's
husband, then on the Russian front.

$\mathscr{F}$OR MY BROTHER
DIETRICH

After weeks of rain the first really luminous, clear fall day! Sissi and I met in the morning in Allenstein at the loading ramp of the freight terminal. Soldiers, vacationers, military transports—a contemporary scene. We saddle the horses while still on the train because both of them are so restless that once released from their confinement they won't stay still for even a moment. We roll up our coats, buckle them, and fasten the saddlebags. And then we and the horses, amid much neighing and snorting, get off the train.

To reach Reussen via Jommendorf, we have to ride through Allenstein diagonally in the direction of Lanskerofen, an exciting stretch, because whenever we meet a truck or a trolley one of the horses is sure to jump clear across the street. Having finally escaped the city, we head south, at first on a blacktop road framed by mountain ash, whose bright red berries confidently and joyfully look up to the azure sky. We manage to get off this asphalt road for a few days even before Reussen, although occasionally and reluctantly we have to get back on it.

In Reussen we climb a steep, sandy road between old wooden houses, and then, before us, autumnal splendor in a whole range of colors—the vast forest complex of southeastern Prussia that we plan to explore. To the left a blue lake surrounded by dark firs, to the right the smoke of potato fires rising up to the sky like a sacrifice to the gods.

Afternoon in East Prussia.

These images—falling leaves, the blueness beyond, the reflection of the autumn sun on the harvested fields—this is life, reality, more so than any one specific act. We are shaped not by events but by what our eyes behold.

I am full of anticipation. What sights still await us in these almost perfect days? Do you also sometimes have the feeling of such closeness, of being separated from something by only a thin veil—but from what, exactly? From

Lake Warien, the fishing rights to which Friedrichstein owned.

insight? From truth? From life? I don't know, but I sense it and wait for it with the sort of certainty with which one waits for a miracle.

It is indescribably beautiful to ride on this sandy soil, the leaves rustling under the horses' hooves—beeches and oaks, and every now and then a lime tree or the reddish trunk of a pine. At the Ustritz locks, between Lake Lansk and Lake Ustritz, we meet a lumberman who shows us the way to the forestry office of Lanskerofen, an incredibly lovely, isolated spot on the western shore of Lake Lansk. The house is new: logs, white with black beams and a steeply sloped thatched roof, adjoining living quarters and stable in the shape of a horseshoe, and a water pump in the middle of the open yard facing the lake. It is quite pretty, perhaps a little bit too deliberately German-peasant style for my taste. We water the horses, and the friendly ranger, home on a week's leave from the Eastern Front, invites us for lunch and gives us a few sightseeing tips for our journey. Following his advice, we decide on the eastern route, particularly since he sent word to his colleague at Hartwigswalde that we would be spending the night there.

This, the northernmost part of the Neidenburg district, is the real Masuria, and probably its poorest section. After Dembenofen, toward Ortelsburg, the soil becomes more brittle, heath and sand, an occasional pine tree, and endless flat hills covered with dry grass. It has an almost Asian feeling, this land. As a matter of fact, according to our map the name of one of the roads that we ride on for quite a stretch is Tatar Road.

It is difficult to find our way here—countless uncharted, rarely traveled crisscrossing trails we cannot coordinate with our map markings. Apparently nobody here follows a marked trail but makes his own, and because the vegetation along these new trails is as sparse as along the old ones, it is an endless maze. Finally—it has by now grown dark—we get to a real road and find the forestry office of Hartwigswalde, where we will spend the night. The ranger and his wife are extremely hospitable. Being from the West, they are somewhat baffled by the people here, largely because of their being so undemanding and lacking in ambition. They say it is difficult to get them to work, for they have little desire for money; they do only as much as is absolutely necessary to survive. Few of their children go into service or move away to make more money. But this is a most attractive trait as far as I am concerned. Strange: those who are well off want to be still better off; only people who know how hard it is to earn a living seem to be content. Here, where an acre yields so little, the small farmer does not have an easy time.

SEPTEMBER 28, 1941

Again blue skies, but today everything is covered with hoar frost. During the night the temperature dropped to twenty degrees; our horses seem off their feed because there are no oats here and the synthetic fodder is not to their taste; this makes us a little uneasy. The forest ranger, riding a fat black horse, accompanied us part of the way through his domain, almost all of it modest growth, but the landscape is lovely. The annual timber yield here is less than half what it is in Quittainen.

Sunday calm has settled over the land and the two small villages we pass. Near Schüttschenofen our guide leaves us at the edge of a large reforested area stretching almost uninterruptedly eastward for about sixty miles to Johannisburg. I have a great deal of affection for this sparse landscape and its people. Strange how the customs of these eastern peoples are everywhere the same from the Baltic to the Black Sea: from Lithuania to the Balkans, one can see the same scenes of grown men or children who day in, day out seem to do nothing but lead their cows along the edge of the road or woods.

I told the ranger that in Slovakia and the Carpathians I often saw peasants walk for hours to market with but one chicken or a chunk of cheese, and he said it was not much different here. Last year he ordered four thousand pounds of potatoes from a peasant, but never got them. When he asked about it, the man answered, "Why should I sell everything at once? What will there be left for me to take to market?"

To give our horses a rest, we decide to walk part of the way in the direction of Lake Paterschoben, more or less by instinct because our map is of no help here. When we emerge from the forest after about an hour's walk, there is the lake, stretched out before us like a Persian miniature: turquoise sky above dark-blue water, and in front a reddish-yellow field. It is sheer joy to ride so carefree and revitalized

through the autumnal land, so remote from all those domestic everyday cares and worries about the future that dog
our every step. Sun and wind, the hoofbeats of our horses on
the sandy road, and the odor of decaying leaves—that is the
world we are now a part of.

It is six miles to the forestry office of Reusswalde where
we plan to eat, and we cover this distance at a more or less
easy pace. Sissi's horse moves with wonderful rhythm,
floating weightlessly over the path, while my intractable
creature stumbles over every pebble and at times over her
own feet.

We have come to a more fertile region; the woods too are
denser and more varied here. Our map now guides us
faultlessly to the forestry office, looming up behind a road
bordered with chestnut trees whose fallen leaves cover the
graveled path like huge hands.

The ranger, a middle-aged bachelor, after feeding both us
and the horses well, escorts us for a stretch. Smoking a big
cigar and enveloped in a cloud of dust, he sits in his yellow
trap between two female relatives from Hamburg who are
staying with him, and drives so rapidly that we have a hard
time keeping up with him. At the boundary of his realm he
takes leave of us and recommends "Aunt Hedwig" in the
neighboring forestry office for our next stopover.

Again endless sandy roads, forests, potato fields, wheat
fields, and more forests, and an occasional village or some
scattered cottages along the road. In the afternoon the
sound of church bells. A carriage with a baby in it, accompanied by numerous godparents, makes its way through the

sand. Later, in the village, we meet the pastor, a skinny little man in a black coat, carrying his priestly vestments in a knapsack on his back.

Shortly after sunset we arrive at the Friedrichsfelde forestry office. Except for Aunt Hedwig, who is herself a guest, there is no one in charge there, so we confer with the coachman, who is more than willing to stable the horses and supply them with enormous quantities of oats. Then I look up Aunt Hedwig to ask her permission to spend the night in the hayloft, not entirely without misgivings because we had been told that she is somewhat ill-tempered and not too tractable. To my delight, she is not at all surprised to have two unescorted ladies on horseback turn up in this godforsaken spot in the middle of the night. She promptly declares that it is much too cold to sleep in the barn, and invites us in. So we get our saddlebags and spend the night in the laundry room on beds with mattresses.

The forestry office is in a very isolated spot, on the edge of a big meadow ringed by woods. The light of the full moon forms a luminous arc above the rising mist, and our thoughts turn eastward. Strange to think that the same light that brightens the silence and isolation of these woods should also be shining over the bloody battlefields of Russia.

When we get back from our evening walk Aunt Hedwig welcomes us with fried potatoes and a much-appreciated cup of hot tea. She has obviously taken a liking to us, and launches into stories about her childhood, about her home on the island of Sylt, about her grandfather who lived there in the 1830s and other relatives who went to sea, and about a neighbor, Numme, who disdainfully dismissed the president and the royal ministers in Berlin, calling them "nothing but servants." "Yes, on Sylt most were captains," Aunt Hedwig tells us with pride; "they knew the world and all the oceans. And they had culture and were refined, educated people, until the vacationers came. Then it was all over, and now Sylt is a sort of New America."

SEPTEMBER 29, 1941

When we start out, we find that everything is again covered with hoar frost and once more the sun rises brilliantly in the clear sky. It doesn't get warmer until about ten o'clock. In front of us lie the huge forests of Friedrichsfelde, Puppen, and Johannisburg; we traverse them from west to east, at times on grassy swards, at others on unmarked sandy trails. In this way we will cover about twenty-four miles, up to Rudzanny.

Shortly after leaving the forestry office we cross the Capacisca, a marshy tract stretching for many miles all the way to Poland. On its edge is a stand of young birches lit by the morning sun, a bit farther on a small tree nursery; after that for many hours we see neither houses nor people, only woods. Coming to a hill we ride up to look out over the endless green expanse, over the golden birches and red oaks. Now and then we see a bird of prey wheeling in the blue sky; some doves fly by.

Around noon we arrive at Kurwien, on Lake Nieder, and turn northward toward the lake region, via Kreuzoven and Rudzanny. The towns here look like real fishing villages.

The lake is lovely, but after Rudzanny it becomes heavily populated—a wide gravel road, telephone wires, and finally even an asphalt highway. Despite our superior anti-civilization attitude, the prospect of a warm lunch wins out over our prejudices, and we stop at the Niedersee casino; we let our horses graze on the meadow, and, basking in the sun, we eat a marvelous cutlet while looking out on the blue lake before us.

About the rest of the day we are a little dubious. We had planned to ride up the east shore of Lake Beldahn—it seems like the more attractive route—but this means that at the end of the lake we must take a ferry to get to Nikolaiken. However, it is highly doubtful that this means of trans-

Fishermen inspecting their catch.

portation will suit our extremely spirited horses. The lake is almost ten miles long, and if we don't manage to get the horses on the ferry we shall have to make a detour of over eighteen miles to get to a place to spend the night. Well, never mind, a day like this is very rare indeed, and the lake is so beautiful that we don't want to part from it.

Sometimes in that peculiar state between dreaming and wakefulness one suddenly gets the feeling of having discovered the secret of life or the essence of existence; I get the same feeling about this lake—that it holds the secret of all lakes. It looms up out of the darkness of the surrounding firs as if out of an ancient legend, transcending the pettiness of human concerns and history, dwarfing the shimmering

The nets are pulled in.

reflection of the landscape on its surface. No one has ever managed to harness it, nor has it ever yielded to anyone. Complete in itself, it stands as the last, unchanging outpost of a world increasingly mutilated by man's utilitarianism. I can see why both Chinese and Greek philosophy call water the basic stuff of all matter, to which only the Creator, by ordering the waters to part, was able to give shape. How puny indeed are we human beings by comparison.

Slowly we ride northward in the waning afternoon sun, often not on a path but along the lake or through the forest bordering the steeply raked shore. The sun turns the trunks of the spruces red and the leaves of the beech trees to every shade of yellow, from shining gold to deep copper. Below us lies the blue lake framed by a slender border of yellow reeds. Lord, how beautiful this world is—could be. . . .

Finally we get to the end of this long spit of land and find ourselves at the ferry, and we become very apprehensive. It's so tiny, just about big enough for one vehicle; girded by low staves, it resembles a floating toy. Even if we do manage to get the horses onto the rattling planks of its floor, the throbbing noise of the motor starting will be another horror. The young man in charge of this contraption shows no sympathy for our discomfort; he just grins. We implore him to start the motor as gently as possible; completely un-moved, he goes on grinning. Later we realize he doesn't understand German.

Much snorting, pulling, patting, and pummeling—the horses finally get on the ferry with leaps that nearly land them in the lake. As a precaution, we had unbuckled the saddlebags so that at least something would stay dry. The

young man meanwhile has raised anchor, and with the help
of a long pole pushes off from the safety of the by now
cherished shore. My mare is so frightened her eyes almost
pop out of her head, and she stares at the receding trees in a
trance. Fortunately she does not really grasp what is going
on. Sissi's horse meanwhile is hopping around like a flea
from left to right, completely ignoring Sissi's comforting
murmurs. And then suddenly the motor starts up with a
loud bang, and puffing and spitting like an infernal machine, the boat sets off on its unsteady course.

So many impressions all at once—too much for our high-
strung horses. They admit defeat, and stand trembling,
meek as newborn lambs, forelegs stiffly extended, not dar-
ing to move. On the newly won shore they climb out much
relieved, after the lad has taken a total of eighty-five pfen-
nigs for this frightening excursion, a charge altogether
disproportionate to the psychic energy expended.

In the course of this time-consuming crossing the sun
has begun to set, and by the time we cross the bridge at
Nikolaiken dusk has settled over the lake and the little
town. There might be a problem with finding a stable. We
dismount on the market square and Sissi sets out to look for
a place to stay. I wait a long time under the trees along the
sidewalk of the town square. Across the square I can see
some faintly lit shops. Men are standing at a bar talking. A
memory wells up in me of an evening scene at Avignon,
with a square and rats in the gutter. God knows why this
vague association stays with me for a while.

As though to legitimize this conjured-up image, an air
sung in French comes to my ears—it's the Toreador Song

from *Carmen*—and then I see the singer, walking across the square driving two head of cattle. Perhaps this captured Frenchman is from the Midi and dreaming of a restaurant at Avignon, of white bread and red wine, of bullfights at Orange, and maybe his vision has infected me. I have no chance to ask him where he is from because at this very moment Sissi comes back with the dread news that no stable is to be found, and because of a shortage of straw, feed, and other staples nobody is willing to take us in.

Eventually we move into a pitch-black stable with neither straw nor anything else, one that Sissi had rejected as utterly unsuitable. We then ring the bell at an inn with a big sign reading "CLOSED DUE TO ILLNESS." Still, the taciturn woman who opens the door is willing to take us in, and since she seems free of any infectious disease we leave our saddles there and set out again in search of food for our horses. After various vain tries, we are guided by our slowly expiring flashlight to the outskirts of the town and into the kitchen of a peasant having his evening soup with his children. He listens to us without saying much, and promises to bring us oats and hay after finishing his own meal.

And, indeed, the good man, carrying a big lantern and accompanied by two boys lugging hay and the long-awaited oats, shows up after our meal of fried potatoes, by then cold, prepared by our hostess. We cross the bumpy square to the stable. The man is enthusiastic about our horses and, like all the people in this region, flabbergasted by their size. They can't be left without straw, he says, and sends the two boys out to get some while he goes down to the lake with us for water.

The town is utterly deserted; not a sound is to be heard. There is no light anywhere and no one out on the street. Yes, the men are all gone, our friend tells us, "only some of us peasants have been given leave for the fall harvest." We exchange a few words about what might still lie ahead of us, discuss the harvest, and bid him goodbye. Either our generous compensation or the beauty of our horses prompts him to show up at the crack of dawn with oats and an offer to groom the horses. By six o'clock, when Sissi in her warm-up suit, our standard nightdress, gets to the stables, everything is already taken care of. The horses are happy and obviously quite satisfied with their food ration. They deserve it; the day before we'd spent ten hours on the road.

SEPTEMBER 30, 1941

Since we heard that Dr. Schilke is staying at a farm called Dommel, only about two miles from Nikolaiken, we decide to go there for our breakfast. By the way, I can understand why the local population was so startled by the size of our horses. As we were riding out of town, I found that from my saddle I had no trouble looking into the attic windows of their tiny houses.

Dommel turned out to be a glorious idea. First of all, the breakfast was excellent, and the site of the farm is absolutely unique. I have never seen anything quite so charming in all of East Prussia. It's about eight hundred acres on a wide spit of land extending about two miles into Lake Spirding. At the edge of the water about halfway down to the end is the farm itself: lovely old buildings, a lime tree in front of a small manor house, and an unfortunately not so nice bigger new house—but it is easy to overlook this flaw considering the phenomenal location and the view, which reaches far across the neighboring Lake Beldahn. A huge old ash tree still in full leaf stands by the blue water, and a well-tended small park runs along the shore.

The house is furnished in late Biedermeier. A small garden room with striped dark-blue wallpaper, white enam-

In spring and autumn the roads were washed out.

eled doors, and painted Biedermeier chairs and easy chairs; watercolors of ancestors in oval frames are tastefully arranged on one wall; facing them a tall blue-and-white vase and some precious china on a table with gilded legs. In the next room there is a sort of platform on which stands a desk next to a potted palm. This is also painted in white and contrasts beautifully with the dark wallpaper—an almost Fontane-like ambience.

The landscape is unforgettably lovely, the true Masuria we got to know on our paddleboat excursions: not too many woods, much water, sandy roads amid an infinite expanse of low hills, red roofs under a cloudless azure sky. We ride for about two hours along the shore of Lake Spirding. It is really enormous, and bluer than would seem possible. The road winds through the land in a leisurely way, sometimes through fields, sometimes a narrow path, then again a real road that links one village to the next, branching off now to the north, now to the south. And everywhere the people are harvesting potatoes. Everybody already or still able to walk is out: children, women, old men. And war prisoners. At Wensen we turn off toward the north, and for the rest of that day and a good part of the next we follow along the Russian positions of the Masurian winter campaign of February, 1915. Even to a layman's eyes it is obvious that this is classic war terrain: a natural twenty- to twenty-five-mile water barrier, with partially tree-covered hilly land providing good cover. Now and then a dominant elevation looms up.

According to our map, the village of Seehöhe at the mouth of Lake Martinshagen, which is about ten miles long and just over a few hundred feet wide, has an altitude of

518 feet. We climb up to the highest point, where a general would most likely position himself, and from there it is possible to look far across the land and see its contours recede on the far-off horizon. To the left the lake borders on a big marsh, and behind us at the edge of a wooded hillside is the soldiers' cemetery of Seehöhe, infinitely remote and isolated. Strange to see that on the old, barely covered-over fortifications of the First World War a new defensive line is being erected: like a wide gray ribbon, the tank barriers wind through the terrain. Barbed wire crisscrosses the landscape; an entire farm at the far end of Lake Türkle is barricaded.

Stopping for lunch in an enchanting stand of birches at the edge of a small clearing, we unsaddle the horses and tether them to a tree. Sissi's inexhaustible store of provisions has yielded up a can of sardines and even some chocolate. And now we are lying on our backs, and the sun, filtered through the leaves, is shining down on our faces.

When I open my eyes I see the blue sky and the white trunks of the young birches. Now and again a leaf flutters silently to the ground. This is the time of ripening and completion, and also the time of leave-taking. How young they all were, our cousins and brothers and friends—and now so much remains unfulfilled, unfinished. Nature is kinder: she sets aside an entire summer for ripening, and presents her riches before taking them back piece by piece and leaf by leaf.

I am reminded of the last confirmation in the little country church at Quittainen. Eight girls in white dresses and six boys in their first blue suits were standing there. I saw them as through a veil, because suddenly it became quite clear to me that none of those boys—unlike their fathers—would ever again stand at that altar and it would be the lot of most of those little girls to remain to fend for themselves. The pastor had chosen as his topic the words "Those others rely on horse and wagon, but we think of the name of the Lord our God." And outside, in front of the church, soldiers were sunning themselves and waiting, waiting to begin their march against Russia on June 21st. Since then we seem to have done nothing but say good-bye—not only to people but to everything else we love: the roads we have ridden on so often, the trees we played under as children, the landscape with its colors and smells and memories.

Sissi's horse is bored and becoming restless, and as he generally dictates the tempo of our trip we saddle up and get started. After some searching we find our way back to the road and the lovely red aspens, and before long, spread out before us, is the wide expanse of land with its brown hills and the sparkling lakes that lie behind them or tucked away in their folds. It is a landscape out of Eichendorff, and the soft breezes echo the yearning and bliss of his poetry.

In the afternoon we ride by a farm—a quiet, sunny farm from which come the rhythmic sounds of a threshing machine. The open gates of the stable beckon invitingly, but there are a good two hours of daylight left and we decide to keep on riding. Then—and this may be the high point of the day—a huge yellow-gold maple looms up in front of us on a gentle slope, outlined against the luminous sky: beginning and end, fulfillment and longing, question and answer, all rolled into one. It stands there like the tree of knowledge.

One ought to stay here. I would never tire of looking at this tree, waiting for its leaves to drop to the ground one by one—beautiful big yellow leaves with red stems. And I remember what Otto Hentig told us about the maple festival in Japan: when the maples turn color the villagers leave their houses and go to the mountains, where they sit down around a maple and look at it, silently and in awe, all day long.

We walk the horses for a while and then, after watering them at Lake Ublick, ride the last couple of miles to the Lindenhof farm, the home of Mr. Bludau, a renowned horse breeder. We assume that he would approve of our excursion and have oats for our horses. It is early evening, as usual a little too late to be arriving anywhere. The steward, keys in hand, is walking across the yard, and bids us see the "gentleman," who lives in an extremely ugly but very big, imposing house. I ring the bell, introduce myself, and haltingly make my little speech. A complete waste of time; the person I am speaking to is a guest, not the lady of the house, and so the ceremonial speech has to be repeated all over again. My diagnosis, Potsdam military aristocracy, turns out to be correct. The lady of the house is very helpful, even very pleased about our visit, and the husband, with cane and plaid breeches, who has meanwhile turned up, is overjoyed when he finds out that Sissi is a Lehndorff—that is to say, from a famous "horse family." Soon the two of them are lost in reminiscences about racing.

The guest rooms, oddly, are numbered, but otherwise everything is quite traditional and by our standards extremely luxurious. There is even hot water and we are able to have a real wash.

In deference to our surroundings I put on my one still clean blouse, which Sissi considers quite unnecessary, but I think our hosts might appreciate it; after five days the blouse I came in is much the worse for wear.

OCTOBER 1, 1941

I think that nowhere in all of Germany can one find so much ready hospitality and spontaneous helpfulness as in East Prussia. We take off in the morning, supplied with sandwiches and many good wishes, and accompanied part of the way by our host riding a small, wonderfully wiry twenty-year-old mare. At Dankfelde our ways part, and we continue straight ahead northward via Kraukeln, circle Lake Kraukel, and then change to a slightly westward course.

After Lake Kraukel the landscape is no longer attractive: flat land, roads, beet fields, until finally we have to lead the horses along a stretch of the Lötzen-Angerburg road while innumerable cars full of military, SS, and other officials rush by.

We decide to take the first road branching off the highway, in the direction of Lake Dargainen, and the afternoon turns out to be wonderful—lots of sand, blue water, gentle hills, and some charming villages. At the edge of a sunny meadow we eat the sandwiches given us by our hosts and take a little nap while the horses graze. Half asleep I can hear their rhythmic chewing and feel them move around on their long leads, until suddenly the big mare snorts in my ear, making me jump out of my skin.

Our trip is nearing its end—only ten miles to Steinort. Once more we climb a hill, overlooking the land between Lake Dargainen and Lake Gall, leaving behind us the freedom of these past days. We arrive at the village of Haarschen and the old cobblestone road, ride past Lorck's house and the Kirsait ferry, and finally come to the long road leading through the Steinort forest. And now here are the old oaks, long gossamer threads float over the paddock—Indian summer has come—and somewhere a cock crows.

LEAVING HOME

It was 3 a.m. I no longer remember the exact date, for the days ran into each other chaotically. But I do know what the time of day was, because I looked at my watch, perhaps out of some need for documentation or perhaps from a feeling of sheer helplessness.

For a week I had been riding along in the stream of refugees wending their way from east to west. Now in the city of Marienburg the stream was apparently being detoured, for I found myself completely alone at the bridge over the Nogat River. This isolation was almost more frightening than the ghostly column of sleds, horse carriages, drays, people on foot or pulling carts that was spreading out over the endless roads of East Prussia, slowly and inexorably, like lava flowing down a slope.

I was standing at the railroad bridge. A single hanging lamp swaying in the wind cast a weak light over its old-fashioned iron struts, which made grotesque shadows. I had reined in my horse, and before its hoofbeats on the loose planks drowned out other sound I heard shuffling steps and a strange rhythmic knocking. At first I couldn't quite make out the source, but then I saw before me three tired figures in uniform painfully dragging themselves across the bridge: one on crutches, one with a cane, and the third with his head bandaged and his left sleeve dangling empty from his coat.

A regional field hospital, they told me, had given its patients the chance to get away if they could under their own steam, but of nearly a thousand wounded men apparently only these three had summoned up enough energy to do so; the rest, after days of transport in unheated trains without food or medical care, had been much too exhausted and listless to follow this desperate advice. Advice? Under their own steam? Russian tanks were only eighteen miles or so from here, and these three could not possibly cover more than a fraction of a mile per hour. In the bitter cold, how long could these exhausted, freezing men hold out?

In the past six months hundreds of thousands of German soldiers had perished miserably, shot or murdered, and these men were sure to suffer the same fate, whether they decided to stay at the field hospital or walk a few more miles westward. The only question, it seemed to me, was whether they were going to die today or tomorrow.

My God, how few in our country had imagined this end to a nation which had gone forth to seize the fleshpots of Europe, to subjugate its neighbors in the East. And who could deny that conquest and subjugation, enslavement of those others for all time, had indeed been the goal? Until a few short months ago it had been dinned into our ears that not an inch of German soil must ever be ceded to the enemy. When the Russians crossed the East Prussian border, we were told that now the population had to stand together, that the Führer had a secret miracle weapon that originally he had been planning to launch against Russia so as to vanquish her once and for all, but that he had decided to deploy it immediately. Final victory was only a matter of will.

Thus the leadership. But what about the reality?

For me the end of East Prussia had come down to this: three dying soldiers trying to drag themselves across the Nogat bridge to West Prussia, and a woman on horseback, whose ancestors had come from the west into the wilderness east of this river six hundred years ago, riding back to the west—six hundred years of history wiped out.

As I said, I no longer remember the exact day all this was happening, but it was sometime in late January 1945. In mid-January the Russians had launched an offensive against a front that was as fragile and brittle as ice in spring. Whole German divisions had been whittled down to a few hundred men. Tank units had scuttled a third of their vehicles in order to have enough fuel for the rest. And there was no one in the leadership—not a single one of all the battle-scarred generals—who had the courage to ignore Hitler's amateurish strategy and take control, to stop at least this last senseless slaughter.

After the first big Russian offensive in July 1944, which had broken through to Memel and then to Trakehnen in East Prussia, Guderian, chief of the General Staff, repeatedly asked Hitler's permission to pull back the thirty divisions still stationed further north, in Kurland. In vain. Three hundred thousand men, with whom contact had long been lost and who were consequently in grave peril, would have been of invaluable help here in East Prussia. Widening the front—the plan of the by no means optimistic General Staff—would have made it possible at least to get the civilian population out of the threatened areas while the front still held. But Hitler stubbornly asserted that he

needed the divisions in Kurland for his big offensive against
Russia in the spring, and that meanwhile they were contain-
ing powerful Russian forces where they were. So they stayed
put, of no help to anyone and running the risk of being
wiped out at any moment.

In any case the Russians had already demonstrated in
July 1944, when they broke through from Vitebsk to the

Storm clouds over the Pregel Valley.

main supply route and penetrated the German front, that a German offensive in the East was no longer feasible. They had cut the German troops' escape route across the Berezina and cost the lives of three hundred thousand German soldiers in the forests east of Minsk. At the same time, some six divisions were destroyed in Vitebsk, Orsha, and other fortified cities.

Everything should have been done to build a new rear defense line, but Hitler clung to his illusions about new offensives and condemned as defeatist all measures that would take account of the actual situation. As late as December 1944, he even decided to move divisions from the already poorly supplied positions in the East to launch the last-ditch Ardennes offensive—a strategic move that all military experts knew to be sheer folly and that soon collapsed. And so it came about that illusions buttressed by the argument "It cannot possibly all have been for nothing" were invoked to forbid the evacuation of the civilian population, including children. The result was this chaotic maelstrom, the coalescing of three huge waves: the retreat of a defeated army, the disorganized flight of the civilian population of which I was a part, and the forward march of an enemy determined to wreak brutal vengeance.

The spring before, an unstoppable stream of refugees had begun pouring into our region, and we had had all summer to figure out how best to prepare for flight. Just as a storm over the lake is preceded by flights of waterfowl seeking shelter on land, so the slowly advancing Russian wave had set in motion a motley mixture of refugees long before we ourselves were forced to start on our way.

The first to come were White Russian peasants with small horses and light carts carrying a few meager belongings and babies, the rest of the family accompanying the carts on foot. The head of the family, with his tall fur hat, walked in front of the cart or next to the horse, holding the reins. A little later came the Lithuanians, then the people from the Memel region, and finally the first group from the easternmost border areas of East Prussia. At that time, the estates and many villages still offered these migrants and their horses shelter, a place to rest and prepare a meal. As emergency conditions became the norm, refugees ceased to be regarded as a novelty even by the curious village children.

I was struck by the fact that most of their carts either lacked adequate protective covering or were so weighted down by heavy rugs that the people could not take along as much baggage as they otherwise might have. That is when I decided that our people should make straw mats and build eight wooden frameworks to use as superstructures on our wagons.

Around the middle of January, a representative of the regional administration appeared at my home to inform me that if I continued in defeatist preparations for flight I could expect harsh punishment. These preparations involved making the straw mats and constructing the wooden frames as protective coverings for our open wagons. The work had been done in secrecy, but apparently some Nazi informer had seen these unusual items in a barn and reported the discovery.

The day after the party official came to warn me and to

proclaim also that there was no reason for any alarm, the mayor was ordered to have all male civilians report to the people's militia immediately. Except for a handful of men exempt from military service for medical or job-related reasons, this order obviously could only have been intended for men over sixty and the disabled. A pall fell over the village. Accompanied by their tearful wives, the men came limping in—lame Marx and half-blind Kather and old Hinz. The mayor handed them Italian rifles and eighteen cartridges each; that's all there was. And then they went out into the freezing night to await their uncertain fate.

The people's militias were supposed to guard the fortifications erected by Gauleiter Erich Koch the summer before. After the failed July 20th coup against him, Hitler had made Koch and the other heads of the eastern districts (Danzig, Posen, Stettin, and Breslau) "Reich Defense Commissars." No sooner had Koch been designated than he took control of the military—or, rather, he put his party functionaries into key military positions. With a great deal of energy and an equal measure of ineptitude, he threw himself into his pet project: digging trenches and building fortifications. He promptly got into a turf war with General Reinhardt, the army commander in the adjacent eastern area.

Koch built these so-called fortifications—most of which collapsed by January—at the very points where the front had ground to a halt in July 1944. General Reinhardt wanted them built in central East Prussia rather than immediately behind his front lines. According to the Gauleiter, however, this was nothing but defeatism, and it wasn't done; so our villagers had to move into snowed-in, half-collapsed slit trenches—and ours was the only area where this was ever done. The desperate women had been right to weep: events moved so rapidly that we had to leave before we could find out whether the men managed to get to their posts.

Two days later—it must have been either the 21st or 22nd of January—I started out early in the morning, riding from farm to farm to check up on things. Everywhere I went I found nothing but problems: at Lägs the tractor driver, exempted because of indispensability, had been called up; at Skollmen the manager. At many of the farms the horses had been requisitioned; and everywhere the prisoners—the only farmhands still left—were becoming restless. The French ones were worried about the general disarray and wondered how they would ever manage to get back home, while the Russians were convinced they would be accused of sabotage for having survived and worked for the enemy instead of slitting German throats.

Toward evening—it was turning dark—I put in another call to the district office that authorized rail travel permits. I asked for a train ticket to Königsberg at six the next morning; I wanted to see to things at Friedrichstein, the other estate I was managing.

For a few seconds I got no answer at all, and then the voice at the other end said, "Didn't you know? The area has to be evacuated by midnight?"

"I had no idea," I answered, not really surprised, though somewhat taken aback. "Where are the Russians?"

"No idea," he said.

"Well, how are we supposed to do it and where should we go?"

In reply the same voice, which had never tired of repeating that the government would take care of everything and that there was no reason to panic, answered: "It's all the same to us—by land, water, or air."

I called a meeting of my staff at the manager's office and told them what to expect. They were completely confused. Having been told over and over again that final victory was a certainty, they simply could not grasp what I was telling them. I gave them detailed instructions on how much—or, rather, how little—they could take with them in the carts, and where and at what time we would meet that night. I made the manager responsible for seeing that my instructions were carried out.

Everybody was crying, and when I looked at Mrs. Durittke, tears came to my eyes, too. Mrs. Durittke, the wife of the farm's tractor driver, was a wonderful, self-confident, unassuming woman. She tended the pigs and took pride in never having missed a day's work. She and her husband had worked hard all their lives so that their children would have it better. Their younger son had died in France; the older one, Karl, had been a sergeant—a strong, reliable, honest man any army would have been proud of. In time, they had thought, he would surely become an officer, and then all their work would be rewarded. But it was not to be. Instead, one day in the fall of 1944, I met Mrs. Durittke walking slowly across the yard with a pail in each hand; the handsome woman looked old, lost, a shadow of her former self. "For heaven's sake, Mrs. Durittke, what happened?" I asked.

She stared at me with lifeless eyes, put down the pails, and, throwing her arms around me, began to sob uncontrollably. "Karl was killed," she said. "We got the news today. Everything is over. It was all for nothing—our entire life."

Now, four months later, she was sitting here, the wife of a man who two days before had marched off with the militia, the mother of two sons who had been killed. Why should she still flee? And where to? Yes, why? I also asked myself. I urged the people standing around me to hurry up, then quickly got on my horse and rode the five miles back to Quittainen. The snow crunched under the horse's hooves, the road was bathed in moonlight, the temperature was way below freezing.

When I got to Quittainen, I found Inspector Klatt, who had already gotten the news, sitting in his office looking glum. In front of his desk stood the local Nazi leader belaboring him about our refugees. Since the fall we had taken in about four hundred refugees from the Goldap region who had started out for the West in October, shortly before the Russians occupied Goldap. When the German troops retook Goldap and Nemmersdorf in November, these people had come to us and were waiting to see what was to become of them. The first documentation of what happened when the Russians occupied a town now began to be circulated. Since we automatically assumed that everything the government printed or broadcast was a lie, my initial reaction was that these pictures from Nemmersdorf were faked. As it turned out, they weren't: women had indeed been stripped naked and nailed to barn doors, and twelve-year-old girls had indeed been raped; sixty-two women and children had been found murdered in their homes, and the pictures of dead women with torn clothes lying in the streets and on compost heaps were not faked.

The refugees from Goldap spent the winter with us, making inroads on our feed supply, but that did not worry me unduly; I knew now that we wouldn't use it up anyway. The Nazi leadership, however, did worry about it, and in early January, with the sound of gunfire within earshot, one of these brilliant thinkers came up with the idea of sending the men and horses all the way back to Goldap, about a hundred and fifty miles from us, to use on the spot the feed stored there. This meant that we were stuck with three hundred and eighty women and children unable to leave with their carts and belongings because their men and horses had been sent off and by now had probably run into the advancing Russian front.

Just two days before all this, I had tried to ward off the inevitable by suggesting to the local mayors that these refugees be allowed to hitch their carts to our tractors and get them out of harm's way as quickly as possible. But the mayors had hundreds of objections—we were going to need the tractors for our spring planting, there was no guarantee that they'd get them back to us in good shape, et cetera—and so nothing came of my suggestion.

Now the local Nazi boss, our former innkeeper, was standing before us and saying he had been instructed to tell us that we had to take the refugees with us. We said that of course was out of the question. We could leave without them only over his dead body, the official answered. Inspector Klatt, a tall, blond, red-cheeked, powerfully built man, got up from his chair, and without another word to the party official left the room. Klatt's agricultural expertise was known throughout the region, and the Nazis would have liked nothing more than to claim him as their own and make him head of their regional farm administration. Twice they had asked him to join the party, alternately cajoling and vaguely threatening, and twice he had somehow managed to turn them down. Klatt and I began to make the rounds in the village imploring people to take only the barest necessities with them, but this advice, and all my careful preparations, went unheeded in the chaos.

Some months before, I had clandestinely made a sort of "mobilization plan" spelling out in detail which men at which estates were to drive which carts, the maximum each family would be allowed to take along, and the absolute minimum needed. I had drawn up maps showing all the country roads and the ferries across the Nogat and the Vistula. I had assumed that crossing the rivers might pose a problem since the bridges were likely to be destroyed by the warring parties. Each estate was supposed to get a number of these maps, but in the chaos, confusion, and desperation, these preparations became completely beside the point. Anyway, it was no longer possible to get in touch with the other estates to implement plans for a joint evacuation. Would we meet with the others? Would we ever meet again anywhere at all?

One last time, for the record, I would like to list the names of the farms and estates, all those lovely names that no one will ever mention again: Quittainen, Comthurhof, Pergusen, Weinings, Hartwigs, Mäken, Skollmen, Lägs,

Amalienhof, Schönau, Gross Thierbach, Klein Thierbach, Nauten, Canditten, Einhöfen.

We had become so accustomed to living with the war and the follies of the Nazis that we operated on two inter-meshing though contradictory levels without really being aware of doing so. I had known since my university days at Frankfurt, when Hitler came to power, that East Prussia would one day be lost. Still we had gone on living as though everything would stay the same, as though what mattered was maintaining and improving the land for future genera-tions, even though we knew that each new building or barn or piece of machinery would only benefit the Russians in the end. It seemed pointless to plan for the future, but we nonetheless continued to pay meticulous attention to every detail, to be upset by a flawed design, an inaccurate invoice, a poorly planted field, and to insist on doing everything as well as we could.

We had known for months that we would have to leave for good. Still, when my sister and her husband and son-in-law (at home on military leave) came for a brief visit one day, we brought out the horse sleds and went hunting. For an entire afternoon we rode silently through the fresh snow and thickets and woods. And everywhere we saw fresh tracks: deer and hare and wild boar. We were after boar, and we tracked our quarry for hours, as though this were just another hunt in ordinary times. Meanwhile we knew only too well that tens of thousands of German and Russian soldiers were bleeding to death in the snow and ice of this merciless winter.

That afternoon my relatives gave me a disturbing bit of

news. (In those days nothing was as important as "being in the know.") Before July 20th, although I was living in a remote part of East Prussia, I was probably better informed than large segments of the local leadership, for they had long ago lost the ability to distinguish between their own propaganda and fact, between illusion and reality. But after July 20th, when all my friends were arrested and I found myself in great trouble, I was without reliable news sources. Now I heard belatedly that the Führer had ordered the arrest of the three most important men in the operational division, men whom we knew personally.

This is how it came about. Sometime in mid-January the northern flank of the Russians' pincer offensive had penetrated from Ostrolenka via Allenstein to Frisches Haff; their advance tanks arrived on January 21st, thereby cutting off East Prussia from the rest of Germany. On January 12th the southern flank at the Baranov front had already begun to move on Warsaw. In the midst of the total collapse of the Eastern Front, when nobody had a clear picture of the situation, Lieutenant Colonel Christen, who was stationed in the operational division at Zossen, received a report from Cracow that Warsaw had fallen. Christen forwarded the report to Lieutenant Colonel von Knesebeck, head of the division, who in turn forwarded it to Colonel von Bonin, head of the signal corps. Alas, the report was premature: Warsaw did not fall for another five days. When Hitler heard about Bonin's report and found out that it was inaccurate, he had the three men arrested. This meant that during the crucial final phase the operational unit was left without leadership. When I heard this—naturally, it had not been made public—it became crystal-clear that the end was not far off. Anyone who in the middle of a crisis had the chief of his operational division arrested and accused of defeatism for passing on a bona fide report must himself be convinced that the end was at hand.

This strange mentality of the National Socialists—to want the impossible, to substitute illusions for strength, and to treat all who did not share these illusions as traitors—reached its apogee during those January days. When the situation was as critical as could be, when the consequences of the insane policies of the country's leadership were obvious to all, the "greatest strategist of all times" began to lash out wildly. Soldiers were shot and generals fired. In those desperate, critical days, when hundreds of thousands of Germans—soldiers and civilians—perished, Hitler replaced general after general: General Reinhardt, the chief of the Northern Army, was replaced by General Rendulic; General Harpe, the chief of Army Corps A, by General Schörner. General Hossbach, commander of the Fourth Army, and General Mattern were also fired. Heinrich Himmler, a man with no experience in strategy, on January 23rd was made commander in chief of the newly formed Army Group Vistula, a unit more imaginary than real.

But to get back to our preparations and flight. I stuffed what I considered the barest necessities into a backpack: some clothing, photographs, and papers. A small saddlebag with toiletries, bandages, and my old Spanish crucifix had been packed some time before. Trudchen, my cook, prepared a quick supper, and she, two secretaries, and I sat down to eat. The older of the two secretaries, the very efficient Miss Markowski, a passionate believer in the Führer who had greeted every victory bulletin with undisguised joy, was very subdued, though I am convinced that she held the doubters and "traitors" responsible for this catastrophe. It was a question that was never to be resolved for her, for this poor soul went to Danzig, where she boarded the *Gustloff*. It was one of four passenger ships berthed at Danzig that were converted to transports and sent to Lübeck when Dönitz ordered the evacuation of as many of the Bay refugees as possible. On January 30th the *Gustloff*, with six thousand refugees and soldiers on board, was torpedoed and sunk by Russian submarines. The same

The snow-covered allée of lindens leading from Friedrichstein.

fate befell the 17,000-ton former luxury steamer *General Steuben*. Crammed with wounded from stem to stern, it was sunk a week later on the way from Pillau to the West.

We sat down to a quick meal. Who knew where the next one would come from? Having eaten, we left the dishes and silverware on the table and for the last time walked out the door, leaving it unlocked. It was midnight. Outside, the people had assembled. I went to the stable, got my trusty horse, and made a point of telling the coachman to hitch my beloved white Draulitter mare to his cart, but in his excitement the old man forgot to do so, so she stayed behind with the other animals.

The distance to Preussisch Holland from Quittainen was only seven miles, normally about an hour's ride. On this night it took us six hours. The roads were iced over, the horses kept slipping, and the coupé, with two sick patients in it, kept skidding. People poured out of side roads, blocking the intersections; then, about half a mile before our destination, everything ground to a complete halt. We stood for two hours without moving forward an inch. Finally I decided to walk into the town to learn what was happening; I was eager to see what the Nazi bosses, who only three days ago had called all preparations for flight defeatist and had threatened severe punishment, were doing now.

I made my way through the mass of vehicles and people to the district party offices. The doors were wide open. Scorched papers were flying about, and discarded files lay scattered on the floor. The rooms were deserted. "Naturally, they're the first to take off, those swine," said a farmer who, like me, was rummaging around among the papers. Yes, they were gone; soon, praise the Lord, they would all be gone. But at what cost! All I could think about was how much we would have been spared these last six months had the attempt of July 20th succeeded.

The town was like a blocked turntable. Tractors and wagons coming in from two sides had stopped everything until it was impossible to move in any direction at all. I went to the post office, and — would you believe it? — the trusty old postal service was working. Chaos reigned outside, the leaders had taken off, but the clerks were at their posts.

What's more, I was even able to place a phone call to Friedrichstein, about seventy-five miles east. There everything was still normal, the sort of abnormal normality that had characterized our life for so long. They had not yet been ordered to evacuate — nor did they ever receive such an order. Anyway it was too late. While we were on the phone, Russian tanks were breaking through to Frisches Haff. East Prussia was cut off, and for those who — unlike us — were not in the western border regions, an evacuation order had become meaningless. Their only possible escape route was the iced-over Gulf of Danzig.

When I got back to our group two hours later, I found them freezing and desperate. Mr. Klatt thought the whole undertaking senseless. "If we're to end up in Russian hands," he said, "then let it be at home." That seemed to be the unanimous sentiment. They also had arrived at another unanimous decision: that I was to try to get to the West on my horse, for the Russians would most likely execute me, whereas they themselves would simply go on milking cows and threshing grain, for the Russians. Neither they nor I had any inkling how mistaken we were to think that nothing would happen to the workers.

No big farewells. I quickly mounted my horse, and while I briefly contemplated whether I should also take the other horse I had brought, a powerful four-year-old chestnut mare, on a lead, a soldier came up to me. Oddly enough, he had a saddle under his arm, and he asked whether he could ride the second horse. So the two of us set out together.

We spoke hardly a word to each other; both of us were preoccupied with our own problems and worries. We rode all day, always with the feeling that we were part of one long line: before us, behind us, next to us, nothing but people, horses, wagons. Every now and then I spied a familiar face or saw the name of a familiar estate on a wagon. Beyond Preussisch Holland we met laborers and shopkeepers pulling handcarts bearing old women or household goods. My God, what a sight! And where did all these people want to go? Did they really believe they could continue like this for hundreds, perhaps a thousand miles?

Night fell. Though we had been under way for more than ten hours, we had not even got as far as Elbing, and progress was becoming more and more difficult. Going from east to west, we were now meeting supply troops coming from the southeast, carrying munitions and equipment on horse-drawn carts. Later we ran into tanks that brutally pushed aside the vehicles carrying refugees into the roadside ditches, where many were overturned and broken.

Then suddenly we were stopped by an officer standing in

the middle of the road, like a rock in a river, on the lookout for deserters. It was dark, but he was able to see that my companion was in uniform. "What leave? There's no such thing anymore." I pleaded with him in vain. The soldier had to dismount, and he disappeared into the night. Now I was left with two horses, riding one and leading the other like a calf to slaughter. I knew I could not possibly continue like this for any length of time. I felt utterly helpless: stopping was out of the question, yet the mare was refusing to move. Suddenly in the darkness I heard someone call my name, and among this mass of refugees I saw three people from Quittainen—one of them Georg, the fifteen-year-old son of our forest ranger—on bicycles. What a stroke of luck! Georg abandoned his bike and got on the horse.

The four of us agreed to meet at a farm I knew just outside of Elbing. When we got there we found the owners gone and the house occupied by soldiers. After a couple of hours' sleep I woke feeling uneasy: the supply troops coming from the southeast had been in such a hurry. It was two in the morning. I roused the others, reshod the horses with new, sharp nails for riding on the icy roads, and went to the soldier manning the phone whom I had seen when we arrived to find out whatever I could about the situation. "What, you're still here? You must leave immediately. We've received orders to blow up the bridge. You'd better hurry if you expect to get across."

Again bitter cold, again a long line ahead of us. After eighteen hours on the road, again only a few hours of sleep, from which I was awakened by a loud, droning voice: "Everybody out, the Russians are here . . ." I have forgotten the name of the village, but it was the last one we had passed through, about two miles back. The house we were in was the mayor's, and he had just received the news. I woke Georg up and we tried unsuccessfully to wake the soldiers sleeping on the floor in the hallway.

Very slowly, in slow motion, as though the images had to be engraved in our minds forever, the beloved landscape passed by us like a backdrop in a surrealist film. Elbing; Marienburg, a town whose history was intertwined with that of my family; and then Dirschau. Dirschau looked like a giant set for an outdoor performance of Schiller's *Wallenstein*: masses of people in outlandish costumes; here and there a campfire, cannon fire close by; at times the houses seeming to tremble. We crawled into a farm building on the outskirts of the town. While one of us tried to sleep on a sofa, the other watched our horses in the stable: a horse was worth a fortune. But we couldn't really rest; people kept walking through the house, picking up a pillow here, a towel there, opening jars of preserved food. We managed, somehow, to have our first decent meal here, in the pantry.

Overcome by the misery around me, I suddenly got the notion that perhaps I ought to turn back with our people. I toyed with the idea of changing course, of perhaps still getting off this westward-moving conveyor belt. It occurred to me that if occasional trains filled with people were going west, an empty one might have to go back east. Perhaps I could get to Königsberg, and from there to Friedrichstein. I went to the station. Here too were thousands of people, but of course no station agent, no information. Finally I found an official. "What—to Königsberg?" He looked as though I had asked him about going to the moon, and he shook his head. No, there were no trains going east anymore.

In Dirschau someone had stolen my fur-lined gloves; I must have put them down for a moment and forgotten about them. It was a hard blow with unforeseeable consequences. There was not a chance of finding another pair, and I certainly could not ride without gloves in this cold. Strange times indeed, when survival hinges on a pair of gloves. Since I was wearing two pairs of ski socks, one on top of the other, I decided to convert one pair to gloves. But the wind whistled through these knitted wraps as through a sieve.

Studying our map, we found westbound back roads and decided to take them to break away from the stream of refugees plodding along at a snail's pace on the main road. Often, when we came to a town where side roads fed into it, or when a wagon broke down, we would spend more time standing still than moving, yet when we tried to outflank the crowd and ride through the fields, we soon found that the snow drifts were too deep. The back roads held the promise of salvation, of escape from this landscape of misery and despair.

At first, everything went fairly well, but every mile took its toll: the horses especially suffered, as repeatedly they became stuck in snow drifts up to their bellies. It grew darker and darker. This landscape of the Kasub—the former Polish Corridor—apparently contained no villages, only scattered little farms, and the people who lived here did not understand German. Then suddenly we could no longer see any road at all. Poor Georg was in misery. He hurt all over; it had been a while since he'd ridden a horse, and his ears were frostbitten. I had frostbite on both hands, and when the sores split open they became extremely painful.

We simply had to find a farm, if only to get some food into our stomachs. I rode up to one of the poor cottages, dismounted, and went in. I found a family at their table, lit by an oil lamp, having their evening soup. They looked at me with alarm. I must have seemed to them to be a fore-shadow of horrors still to come. Communication was diffi-cult, but at least I learned that there was a big farm about two miles from their house. Finally the man got up, took the lamp hanging by the stable door, and walked with us across the hill to the neighboring cottage, whose owner shep-herded us over the next hill, and there indeed we could see the road to a big farm.

The owner was a man named Schnee. We found plenty of oats, and as to sleeping facilities, they were on the floor of the living room, where about twenty people were already bedded down, all of them apparently from the Corridor or Warthegau, and most seeming to know one another. They talked about the time after the First World War when, so they said, Polish atrocities were not unheard of. After mak-ing myself very unpopular by holding forth about *German* atrocities, I soon fell asleep.

Sadly my slim hope of possibly finding a pair of gloves at the Schnee farm was dashed. Everything that could be spared had already been given away, but someone did come up with a piece of drapery material, a needle and thread, and I spent half a day fashioning gloves. Georg became the lucky recipient of a fur hat, white cloth outside, fur in-side—lucky indeed, because the days ahead were worse than anything that had gone before.

The temperature continued to drop, and in addition galelike east winds, very rare in this freezing weather, had begun to kick up. Finally we were ready to leave the farm, and as we rode down a protected sunken lane we saw in the distance, on the road beyond the field, the long file of people still plodding along. Though it wasn't snowing, the air was full of whirling, blowing snow, and as through a heavy white veil, we saw this miserable throng slowly, slowly moving on, pushing against the wind. The frames of many of their wagons had broken. As we joined this ghostly procession, we had our first view of bodies lying along the road. No one had the strength or the time to bury them.

That is how we progressed for days and weeks. From all sides vehicles and people continued to swell the columns of refugees—and not only here in northeastern Germany. Since the autumn, these scenes of long lines of wagons and people were being replayed in the southeast as well. From Bessarabia and the Banat, from Transylvania, from ancient German settlements, the stream of miserable humanity continued to push westward. Behind them their homelands were going up in flames, and those who had decided to stay had long since met their fate. In Transylvania seven hundred years of history were being wiped out.

These scenes will stay with me forever. At one point somewhere along the way—I think it was between Bütow and Berent—you could see straight forward and back along the road in both directions for a three-mile stretch. Nowhere could I see the road itself, only carts, horses, people, and misery. Nobody spoke. All that could be heard was the sound of wagon wheels crunching on the snow.

Another image comes to mind. We must still have been in East Prussia when one day we saw three tanks loaded down with refugees—women and children carting parcels and suitcases, civilians and military men together—a unique, unforgettable amalgam of the ordinary and the extraordinary, of destruction and the will to survive. An eerie sight. For some reason or other they paused for a moment, and a peasant spoke up: "Why aren't you stopping the Russians instead of pushing us off the road?" he asked. One of the soldiers, a fierce-looking character, yelled back, "Because we've had enough of this shit."

Once when we happened to be moving a bit more purposefully, we came upon French prisoners, hundreds and hundreds of them, maybe even thousands. Some were pulling cardboard suitcases nailed to wooden slats. They spoke not a word. The only sound was the scratchy, scraping noise of boxes and suitcases—and all around the infinite snow-covered landscape, a scene reminiscent of the retreat of the Grande Armée more than a century ago.

And still another unforgettable picture. We had been under way for about two weeks when we got to Varzin, the big estate in the district of Rummelsburg which Chancellor Bismarck had acquired as part of his award upon his retirement in 1866: magnificent woods and a model agricultural estate. Having left the Nogat and the Vistula behind us, I thought that we might be able to stop for a while: finally to have arrived at a destination—an intoxicating thought. We rode our horses through the park gate up the slight incline to the castle. There, in front of the center door, stood two drays and two big farm wagons packed with wooden boxes. Well, I thought, some other refugees must have got here ahead of us; I hope there's still room. To my great surprise, I learned that what I was looking at was not the baggage of some East Prussians but the evacuation of the Bismarck archive. So here too everything was being vacated. And I had thought that with the Vistula behind us things would be calm.

Bismarck's daughter-in-law was still alive—a tiny, fine-boned, highly amusing old lady who in her youth had raised many an eyebrow: renowned for her wit, she had ridden to hounds and smoked cigars. She was still extraordinary, so fascinating that I could not tear myself away and leave the next morning as I should have. We stayed for two memorable days. Outside, the refugees were still slowly dragging themselves across the land, and as they passed they were joined by the local population, now refugees themselves.

The cart we had seen when we arrived left without the aged countess. No amount of warnings and arguments would persuade her to leave Varzin. She had no illusions about surviving the entry of the Russians, nor did she want to witness it. She had had a grave dug in the garden, for she assumed that later on nobody would have time to do so. She was determined to stay at Varzin and enjoy its beauty to the very last. And she did just that, in style. In the house itself nothing was changed. Her old butler, who also refused to leave, served at table. We drank bottle after bottle of superb vintage wine, the stuff of dreams. Not a word about what was happening outside or what lay ahead. Animated and witty, she told stories about her father-in-law, about the Imperial court, about the days when her husband, Bill Bismarck, was President of East Prussia.

When I finally bade her goodbye and rode down toward the garden gate, I looked back one last time. She was standing at the door lost in thought, waving a tiny handkerchief. I am not sure, but I think she was smiling.

A few days later, still in Pomerania, we arrived again at a big estate, early one evening. I dismounted, walked up the outside stairs, and rang the bell while Georg held the horses. The owner had obviously seen the two figures and their horses through the window. I was wearing a tall black fur hat, and my belted greenish fur-lined coat might have been mistaken for an officer's coat. It was an old travel coat of mine which I had transformed into a riding coat, with the help of a pocketknife, by slitting it in the back from hem to waist.

It took quite a while before anyone came to the door. When someone finally appeared, it was the owner himself, looking pale and distraught. I told him who I was, and still he said nothing, no invitation to come in. Then suddenly he turned around and called out, "It's not the Russians!" whereupon the entire family, reassured, came down and we exchanged rumors, for neither they nor I knew what actually was going on.

The house was full of refugees: relatives, acquaintances, uninvited guests like us. A big group gathered at the dinner table by candlelight; electricity had been cut off some time ago. Our host, at the head of the table, said grace, and rather ceremoniously began to serve the soup. Everything—every gesture, every word, even the silences—was colored by the grief of leave-taking.

East of the Vistula the houses and sheds where we had found shelter for a few hours or a night had already been vacated, but here in Pomerania everything was still intact— or, at least, what then passed for intact. However, the people feared that what had happened to us would happen to them, though I did not think that the Pomeranians might also have to flee. Neither they nor I suspected on that day in mid-February how soon their turn would come. On February 26th, General Zhukov launched his Pomeranian offensive. By February 28th his tanks, riding roughshod over refugees and residents alike, had advanced to Köslin and Schlawe. The German tanks that were supposed to halt the Russians had only ten grenades each. Their crews were bone-tired and hopeless. For every German tank there were ten Russian ones.

Some of the people in Pomerania seemed almost envious as they waved us goodbye. I am sure that many would have liked to send their children and young women and valuables along with us. But their situation was the same as ours had been earlier in East Prussia: leaving was strictly forbidden, and since every village had its self-appointed patriots ready to denounce their neighbors, no one dared disobey. Never before had there been a national leader who had served the cause of his adversary so well; never before had a commander in chief, by his amateurish strategy, been personally responsible for the deaths of hundreds of thousands; never before had the actions of a man claiming to be the father of his country led his nation to slaughter and closed off all avenues of escape. The man who had told the world that Germany's living space was too small and set forth to expand it robbed millions of Germans of their age-old homeland and shrunk German space to a minimum. Long before the outbreak of the war a joke made the rounds in Berlin that had Stalin refer to Hitler as his Gauleiter.

At the Oder River, German troops tried to dynamite the ice to make something like a tank barrier. They failed. Then they tried to saw through the ice—as with the ice-making technique I remember from my childhood. That too did not work. At these temperatures the ice blocks simply froze together again in solid sheets before they could be pulled from the river.

When we finally arrived on the outskirts of Stettin, there was so much gunfire close by that it would have been pointless to try to get out of this mousetrap. We decided to follow the course of so many others on the road and go all the way up to the coast, ride across the islands of Usedom and Wollin, and then through Lower Pomerania to Ucker-mark. At one point we joined forces with three officers who were familiar with the terrain and were making for the same destination I was aiming for in the hope of finding some members of my family. Escaping at last from the roads crowded with refugees and vehicles, our horses, inspired by the company of other horses, managed about a hundred miles in three days. But when we finally arrived at the Uckermark estate late at night we found all the buildings—the house, the barns, the sheds—occupied by eight hun-dred Polish officers who had got there before us. These poor souls had spent years in some huge prison camp and, while being evacuated from it, had been caught up in the Russian advance, with twelve hundred Polish officers being taken prisoner; our more fortunate comrades were not very optimistic about the fate of their erstwhile fellow prisoners, and their only thought was to get to the West. Who had not been sucked into this maelstrom of disaster?

Rarely have I looked forward so passionately to anything as I did to the reunion with my sister-in-law and her children. I had been also dreaming for weeks of a bath and a change of clothes, for I had ditched my cumbersome backpack soon after starting on this trek. And now here I was, only to learn that three days earlier the family had left, had fled. I could not get it into my head that people were fleeing from here, near Prenzlau, as well. Where would they all go? What would they live on?

So we continued on our way—the word "arrival" no longer was part of our vocabulary. We kept going, through Brandenburg, Mecklenburg, Lower Saxony, to Westphalia. I had made my way across three major rivers that had once defined the borders of our east German homeland: the Vistula, the Oder, and the Elbe. I had started out when the moon was full, traveled through a new moon, another full moon, and still another new moon.

When I had ridden off in the depth of winter it was 20°C below zero, and when I finally arrived at the Metternichs in Vinsebeck, Westphalia, it was spring. The birds were singing. The plows stood ready in the dusty fields. Everywhere the signs of a new beginning. Was it possible for life to go on as though nothing had happened?

It took me a long time before I was able to accept what

happened afterward: the loss of my home. For years, against all logic, I continued to hope for a miracle, even though my political sense should have told me that this is an area in which miracles are not likely to happen. Still, it is possible to accept reality yet continue to dream. However, eventually I became convinced that if we are to put an end to conflicts and expulsions we must renounce the use of force. Before arriving at this conclusion I had wholeheartedly believed in the renunciation of force but not of territory, as Poland demanded. I reasoned that if Poland did not believe our renunciation of force they were not likely to give credence to our renunciation of territory. However, in 1970, when Willy Brandt's government came to power and embarked on an activist *Ostpolitik* such as I had been advocating since the late 1950s, my old temporizing approach no longer seemed defensible. If we want normalization, then it is essential that the border question be resolved once and for all. When did I arrive at this painful conclusion? It is never easy to say precisely when an idea reaches fruition. In this instance, however, I am able to fix the time because I have it black and white, in the preface of a book of mine published in 1962:

> When it became increasingly clear that the implacable position of saying yes to the renunciation of force but no to the renunciation of territory was no longer acceptable because what is needed now is either a yes or a no, I realized that an unambiguous position was required of me emotionally as well. I chose the painful alternative of the positive yes because the negative no would have meant revenge and hatred.

I also do not believe that hating those who have taken over one's homeland, and denouncing those who have chosen the road of conciliation, necessarily demonstrates love for the homeland. When I remember the woods and lakes of East Prussia, its wide meadows and old shaded avenues, I am convinced that they are still as incomparably lovely as they were when they were my home. Perhaps the highest form of love is loving without possessing.

Friedrichstein in the winter.

A Note About the Author

Marion, Countess Dönhoff was born on Friedrichstein, in East Prussia, in 1909. She joined the editorial staff of *Die Zeit* after World War II, became its editor in 1968, and has been its publisher since 1973. She is the author of numerous articles and studies in European history and politics and has received honorary degrees from Smith, Columbia, and the New School.

A Note on the Type

The text of this book was set in Berkeley Oldstyle, a
typeface designed by Tony Stan based on a face originally
developed by Frederick Goudy in 1938 for the
University of California Press at Berkeley.

Composed by Sarabande Press, New York, New York

Printed and bound by Halliday Lithographers,
West Hanover, Massachusetts

Designed by Iris Weinstein

DATE DUE			